TOYS

of the '50s, '60s and '70s

Kate Roberts and Adam Scher

with contributions by Robert J. Smith III

MINNESOTA
HISTORICAL
SOCIETY PRESS

www.mhspress.org

The Minnesota Historical Society Press is a member of the Association of American University Presses.

Manufactured in Canada

10 9 8 7 6 5 4 3 2 1

♾ The paper used in this publication meets the minimum requirements of the American National Standard for Information Sciences—Permanence for Printed Library Materials, ANSI Z39.48-1984.

International Standard Book Number

ISBN: 978-0-87351-927-4 (paper)
ISBN: 978-0-87351-941-0 (e-book)

Library of Congress Cataloging-in-Publication Data
Roberts, Kate, 1959–
    Toys of the '50s, '60s, and '70s / Kate Roberts, Adam Scher.
       pages cm
    Summary: "Toys from the 1950s, '60s, and '70s capture the joy of play and the pure fun of being a kid. But beneath those iconic names are rich veins of nostalgia, memory, and history. These toys—and the stories of the kids, parents, child-rearing experts, inventors, manufacturers, and advertisers they affected—reflect the dynamism of American life"— Provided by publisher.
    Includes bibliographical references and index.
    ISBN 978-0-87351-927-4 (paperback) — ISBN 978-0-87351-941-0 (ebook)
    1. Toys—United States—History. 2. United States—Social life and customs. I. Title.
    GV1218.5.R6 2014
    688.7'2—dc23
                          2014005172

ROBERT J. SMITH III is a PhD student in the Department of American Studies at the University of Minnesota. He earned a Bachelor of Arts degree in Africana Studies and Gender and Sexuality from Brown University in Providence, Rhode Island.

This and other Minnesota Historical Society Press books are available from popular e-book vendors.

For Mary Pat, Eileen, and Rob, my first and still best playmates
—Kate Roberts

For my brothers Robert and John, forever young at heart
—Adam Scher

Contents

Introduction   2

The 1950s   12

The Game of Cootie   17
American Flyer Trains   21
Erector Set   25
View-Master   29
Betsy McCall Paper Dolls   33
Sweet Sue   37
Raggedy Ann and Andy   41
Ike-A-Doo   45
Matchbox and Hot Wheels   49
Davy Crockett Coonskin Cap   53
Revell Model Kits   57
Skaneateles Train Set   61
Electric Football   65
Alpha-1 Ballistic Missile   68
Poor, Pitiful Pearl   72

The 1960s   76

Trolls   83
Robot Commando   87
Barbie   91
Mouse Trap   95
Thingmaker   99
Easy-Bake Oven   103
Rat Fink   107
Tonka Trucks   111
Frisbee   115

G.I. Joe   119

Twister   123

Spirograph   127

See 'n Say   131

Big Wheel   135

Julia Doll   139

The 1970s   144

Uno   149

Baby Tender Love   151

Play Family Castle   155

Lil' Chik Bicycle   159

Jarts   163

Johnny Horizon Environmental Test Kit   167

NERF Ball   171

McDonald's Familiar Places Play Set   175

Sesame Street Wood Blocks   179

Holly Hobbie   183

Six Million Dollar Man
    and Bionic Woman Action Figures   187

Little Professor and Speak & Spell   191

Pet Rock   195

Star Wars Action Figures   199

Simon   203

Image and Source Credits   208
Toy Trademarks   210
Acknowledgments   211
Index   212

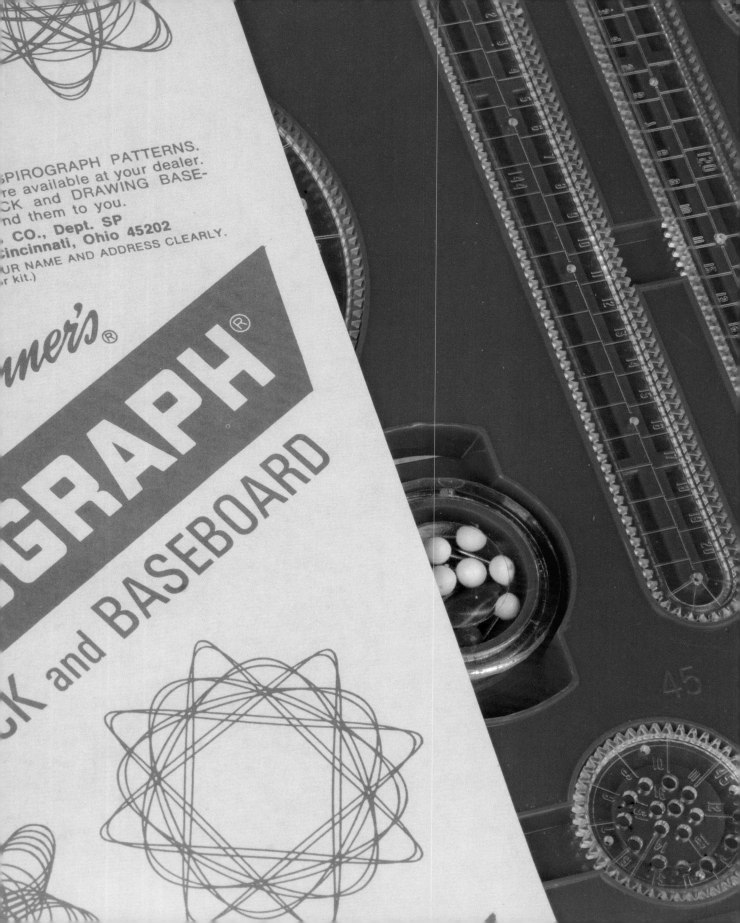

of the '50s, '60s and '70s

Introduction

Kate Roberts

Among the many topics related to baby boomers, there is no shortage of books about our toys. Books highlighting the top toys of the generation. Books on collecting everything from trolls to Hot Wheels to *Star Wars* figures. Memoirs laced with descriptions of toys, those owned and those coveted. Yet over the months we spent developing this book and its accompanying exhibit, even casual references to our topic prompted questions, stories, and plenty of reactions along the lines of, "Wow—I haven't thought about [insert toy name here] in years!" A social media campaign evoked a flood of stories, many of which are included in the following pages. We heard from boomers looking back on childhoods in which they owned few, if any, toys. We've heard about the intense gratification of receiving the top toy on a list during a memorable birthday celebration. Some describe themselves as the last in a long line of siblings who played mostly with hand-me-down toys. Others recall rejecting indoor toys in favor of hours spent on a bike, a Big Wheel, or a skateboard.

The specifics may vary, but the overall enthusiasm for sharing thoughts about toys and childhood is undeniable. Historian Mark Rich (*Warman's 101 Greatest Baby Boomer Toys*, 2005) captures this attitude in his description of boomers' reactions to that Holy Grail of childish covetousness, the *Sears Wish Book:*

> Somewhere in this country, at least one person will stand up for each item in that fabulous catalog and will tell you how that particular item belongs on anyone's list of 101 great toys of their time.
>
> That toy was the greatest ever, they would say. They will stand up for that toy, and they will be right to do so. How

could they be wrong, after all? They were there. They saw, they yearned, they held, they played. If they did not play with their own toy, they played with a friend's. If they never played with it in their own grubby hands, then they carried TV ads and jingles in their minds for years and played with the toys in their heads.

The cynical among us might dismiss this enthusiasm as evidence of boomers' fascination with the nuances of their precious lives. But that's far too simple an explanation. The fact is, the '50s, '60s, and '70s saw a huge increase in the number and variety of toys available to American children. The evolution of toys during that thirty-year period, from the Lionel trains and Tiny Tears dolls of the 1950s to the Atari game systems and *Star Wars* figures of the late 1970s, is nothing short of astonishing. And many of those toys are direct reflections of what was happening in the larger context of American society. They reveal kids' and parents' thoughts, feelings, fears, and aspirations. "Nothing is more natural than that a toy should reflect the life of its period," wrote British novelist and historian Antonia Fraser in *A History of Toys* (1966). And nothing is more natural, it seems, than memories of childhood inextricably interwoven with memories of toys. In a very real sense, toys are us.

To understand how the toy boom occurred during the boom years, we need to venture back in time. Anthropologists and archaeologists have found evidence of toys dating back to the earliest cultures, of course. Play is not a modern concept. Rather, it's the significance attached to children and their play that has evolved over time. British philosopher John Locke is often credited as one of the first to recognize the importance of play in molding children and honing their natural skills. In 1693 he wrote that "it must be permitted Children not only to divert themselves, but rather to do it after their own fashion . . . Gamesome humour which is wisely adapted by nature to their

age and temper, should rather be encouraged to keep up their spirits and improve their strength and health, than curbed and restrained." A century later, Jean-Jacques Rousseau advanced the revolutionary notion that children were more than miniature adults. "Nature wants children to be children before they are men," he wrote. "If we deliberately pervert this order, we shall get premature fruits which are neither ripe nor well-flavoured, and which soon decay."

As time went on, notions of play as children's "work" gained strength, with educators and others touting the importance of proper childrearing techniques, including the choice of toys, in shaping tomorrow's productive citizenry. But it wasn't until the advent of industrialization, as home-based work gave way to factory jobs and everyone, including children, began to have a bit of leisure time on their hands and a bit of expendable cash in their pockets, that the modern era of toys dawned. First in Germany and France, and eventually in the United States, manufacturers began applying the techniques and materials of mass production to the manufacture of toys. Tin was pressed into phalanxes of toy soldiers. Porcelain was formed into exquisite doll heads. The production of toys, like so many other things, was moved out of the home and into the factory.

By the late 1800s, the groundwork had been laid for the toy extravaganza of the boomer era. In the United States, forces of production and consumption fueled the rise of department stores and mail-order houses where more and more modestly priced goods were available. Mass-marketing was a reality, and advertising was an increasingly cutthroat industry. Retailers acknowledged the link between Christmas gift-giving and increased sales, and extravagant window displays featuring the season's must-have toys flanked the entrances of department and specialty stores. Perhaps most importantly, parents (particularly women) were being told by educators, clergy, and child-rearing experts that their highest calling in life was to raise intelligent, moral young men and women.

Fast-forward, then, to the years following World War II, when the birth rate soared, housing starts exploded, and consumer spending increased accordingly. Young middle-class parents created intensely child-focused households, and as young families grew, so did toy sales. Historian Howard Chudacoff describes the situation in *Children at Play: An American History* (2007): "The nation's economic growth in the quarter century after World War II had created an attitude that everyone, especially a child, was entitled to a good life, and thus parents, eager to see their offspring happy and well-adjusted, found it difficult to resist the profusion of commercial playthings that their kids said they wanted. What they wanted were toys."

Add to this mix several more key developments—the availability of materials, especially plastics, that could be made into a variety of appealing toys with equally appealing prices, the rise of imported toys, especially from Japan, and the game-changing role of television in marketing toys to children—and the toy boom starts to seem almost inevitable.

But as we sifted through the stories shared with us in the course of this project, we discovered that some memories took

us away from the world of manufactured playthings and into another realm entirely. Here's one example:

> **Canned goods, Grain Belt, and Monopoly money.**
> *Sure, we received a toy or two on our birthdays and at Christmas, like the year when my sister and I both received an Easy-Bake Oven. We had toys, but one of our favorite games, "Town," was played with none of them. We played Town in our basement with a half dozen or more kids from our family and the neighborhood. We had a Town Store called "Most's," after the nearby grocer. Most's sold eggs (empty egg cartons), butter (empty butter cartons), and canned goods and homemade pickled food from our cellar. We had a school, a restaurant— and a saloon, with empty Grain Belt bottles and a bottle of Canadian Club. We paid for our food and drink with Monopoly money. And we had a police station with a sheriff who arrested the boys who left the saloon without paying for their drinks.*
> ROSE SHERMAN, b. 1958, chief information officer

When all is said and done, some of the most vivid memories of childhood play aren't tied to the toys we owned or coveted. Instead, they're tied to that time in our lives when we had the freedom and the peer support to let our imaginations run wild. We

all know that manufactured toys can spark imagination—just ask anyone who has ever spent hours playing with Barbies or building LEGO worlds. But we also know that kids have the capacity and the motivation to make anything into a toy, and to use their improvised toy in ways we would never have anticipated.

"Play is the work of children," wrote developmental psychologist Jean Piaget. He, along with physician and educator Maria Montessori and many others concerned with the development of children, devoted serious attention to how and why children play. Historian Steven Mintz provides a useful summary of their findings: "Children's play, despite changes in form, remains what it has always been: a way for kids to hone their physical skills, nourish their imagination, rehearse adult roles, conquer their fears, and achieve a sense of mastery." Kids play because they want to, but also because they need to, as a way of making sense of the world and finding their place in it. In this view of the role of play, manufactured toys are optional.

"Kids start out with one power that puts all the rest to shame," writes Mark Rich. "The power to imagine things." I can't read that statement without thinking about a game I often played with my older brother. We called it "Going to Guam," after we saw that place-name on a car's license plate and asked our dad for a quick rundown. I remember being deliciously confused by the presence of this car, apparently from a place you couldn't drive to, in our home town on the Minnesota–North Dakota border. Our game consisted of scaling from one end of our backyard swing set to the other without touching ground (ground being, of course, the coursing waters that separated us from whatever we imagined the island of Guam to be). I don't recall whether either of us ever actually made it all the way to our destination—was there a way to win our game? What sticks with me now is that our game—like most games, like the best kinds of play, like childhood itself, really—was all about the journey.

Featured in this book are forty-five toys popular in the United States in the 1950s, '60s, and '70s. How did we choose which toys to write about? As you flip through the pages, maybe our methods will become clear. We included some classics—toys that everyone associates with boomers—but we countered them with lesser-knowns whose stories of invention or impact intrigued us. We tried to provide a good range of types, from dolls to building toys to electronics and more. We exercised our prerogative and—good boomers that we are—we picked a few toys simply because we remember and love them. Some of the toys pictured date from their debut year. Others are more popular, recent, or recognizable versions of toys from the boomer era. In short, we tried to provide a good mix to spark recognition and jog memories. If we've left you digging through your closets to find your old toys, rifling through albums for photos of birthday parties gone by, or asking yourself what you would have included in this book, we've done our job.

Builds Giant Ferris Wheel

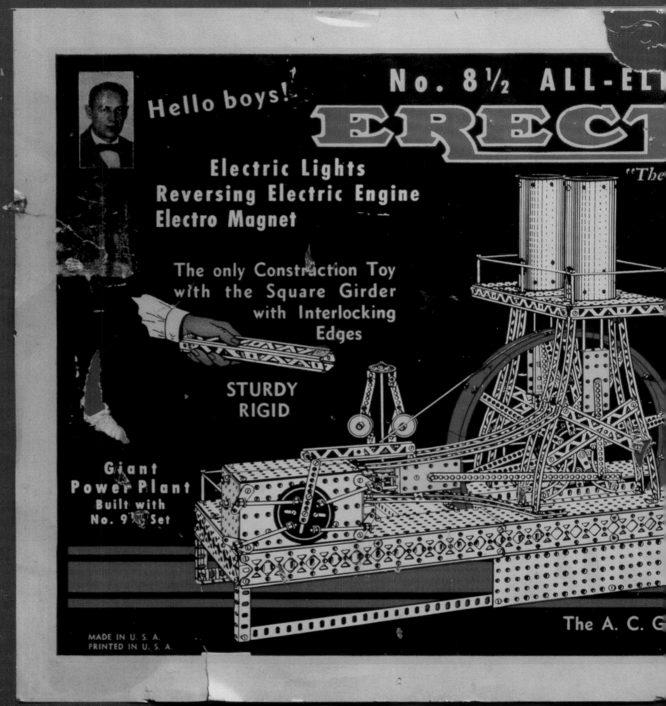

Hello boys!

No. 8½ ALL-EL...
ERECT...

"The...

Electric Lights
Reversing Electric Engine
Electro Magnet

The only Construction Toy
with the Square Girder
with Interlocking
Edges

**STURDY
RIGID**

**Giant
Power Plant**
Built with
No. 9½ Set

MADE IN U. S. A.
PRINTED IN U. S. A.

The A. C. G...

RIC
OR

"'s greatest toy"

Ferris Wheel
Built with
No. 8½ Set

Company   New Haven, Conn., U.

The 1950s

Robert J. Smith III

For many Americans, the 1950s were the nation's heyday, the good old days, the calm before the storm of the '60s. The United States had emerged from the Second World War a global power, albeit one locked in a cold war with the Soviet Union. Economic growth and robust government spending swelled the ranks of the middle class, while a new interstate highway system and easy credit fueled an expansion of the suburban consumer economy. Suburbanites aspired to the ideal nuclear family, complete with breadwinning husband, homemaking wife, their washed-and-pressed children, and a comfortable home full of modern appliances. It might seem obvious to us now that the affluent *Ozzie and Harriet* ideal was never the rule and that the façade of the decade is a trick of our collective memory. During the '50s, abundance for some depended upon the exclusion of others and conformity was tempered by simmering rebellion.

At a 1959 exhibition on American culture in Moscow, Vice President Richard Nixon proudly boasted about the nation's quality of life to Cold War rival Soviet Premier Nikita Khrushchev. Nixon elevated the humble washing machine to an object of geopolitical importance when he showed off a model suburban home with clearly delineated roles for men and women. In this famous "kitchen debate," Nixon bragged that the nation's wash-

1950

Senator Joseph McCarthy accuses the State Department of harboring 205 communists, initiating the "Second Red Scare."

1951

The Marshall Plan expires after spending over $13 billion to rebuild war-torn Europe following World War II.

ing machines were designed to make household chores easier for American women, leaving them with more time to fulfill the other duties expected of homemakers. He imbued an everyday household item with interconnecting notions of gender, consumerism, and foreign policy. In Nixon's hands, the American home was a potent weapon in the Cold War, the American nuclear family cast as patriot, diplomat, and consumer rolled into one.

Many everyday people adhered to this strict formula while finding releases elsewhere—on the leather sofas of psychotherapy offices or in the urban bachelor escapism of *Playboy*'s pages. Betty Friedan spoke to many of the nation's middle-class women. In 1957, she began interviewing her female college classmates in honor of their fifteenth reunion, only to find that many were dissatisfied with their lives as suburban housewives and mothers. With that, she began research on *The Feminine Mystique,* a landmark book that dedicated hundreds of pages to that "strange stirring, a sense of dissatisfaction, a yearning that women suffered in the middle of the twentieth century in the United States," what Friedan called "the problem that has no name." All was not so calm on the home front.

While adults were encouraged to support the nation through consumer spending, American teenagers, moving on from their childhood toys, forged a national youth culture in the 1950s by consuming products—magazines, music, celebrities, and, of course, television—meant just for them. More than any other creature comfort of the suburban ideal, the television has had

1952
After over five decades of colonial rule by the United States, Puerto Rico becomes a self-governing commonwealth.

1953
Marilyn Monroe covers the inaugural issue of Hugh Hefner's *Playboy*, which sells for fifty cents.

1954
The U.S. Supreme Court rules in *Brown v. Board of Education* that "separate but equal" schooling is unconstitutional.

the most lasting impact. A technology both for bringing the family together and for catering to the desires of each member, the medium spoke to a mass audience and also gave young people an outlet to experience the world on their own terms.

Hosted by Dick Clark and filmed in Philadelphia, *American Bandstand* became a youth culture milestone when, beginning in August 1957, it was the first daily television program targeted to teens nationwide. A new national youth culture was under formation with every spin and swivel recorded at WFIL-TV and beamed across the country. *Bandstand* offered young Americans the veneer of freedom and the validation that the culture they produced was mainstream entertainment. Despite its assertion of freewheeling teens, the show was decidedly invested in respectability, a carefully controlled performance of youthfulness. There were strict rules for dancing: not too close or too lewd, and certainly no mixed-race couples. Some *Bandstand* veterans have mentioned that it was taboo to talk about homosexuality or sex of any kind. At the same time that teen-targeted television gave '50s youths refuge outside of the nuclear family's strictures, teen culture was still disciplined by their TV parents Dick Clark and his producers. In speaking to its eager young audience, *American Bandstand* reinforced mainstream culture's message to youths to be sexually restrained and to resist genuine integration, despite the protests of black youths and the show's own veneer of racial integration.

A generation had learned to consume for their families, for their nation, and, through the development of a national youth

1955

Ray Kroc opens his first McDonald's in Des Plaines, Illinois, while Disneyland debuts in Anaheim, California.

1956

President Dwight D. Eisenhower authorizes the construction of 41,000 miles of interstate highways.

culture, for themselves. The kids of *American Bandstand* would become both the radicals of the 1960s social movements and the suburban warriors of the New Right. Below the surface of conformity that defined the 1950s, change had been brewing all along. The unity had been an illusion. Right there in the seemingly calm environs of the nation's suburban living rooms, the seeds of rebellion were being sown. In the quotidian acts of teenagers tuning into *American Bandstand* or, indeed, of black youth protesting for their inclusion, the inheritors of the nation conformed to the consumerist mainstream while slowly pushing the envelope. The words of legendary designer Charles Eames had ricocheted throughout the culture: "Take your pleasure seriously," he famously quipped. Women, people of color, LGBT people, immigrants, and a whole host of diverse groups would embrace that charge—to create spaces of their own making. In the explosion of social movements, consumer cultures, and artistic production since the 1950s, Americans of all stripes have done just that.

For Further Reading

Lizabeth Cohen, *A Consumers' Republic: The Politics of Mass Consumption in Postwar America*

Matthew F. Delmont, *The Nicest Kids in Town: American Bandstand, Rock 'n' Roll, and the Struggle for Civil Rights in 1950s Philadelphia*

Betty Friedan, *The Feminine Mystique*

Elaine Tyler May, *Homeward Bound: American Families in the Cold War Era*

Bill Osgerby, *Playboys in Paradise: Masculinity, Youth, and Leisure-Style in Modern America*

1957
Philadelphia-based *American Bandstand* becomes the first daily television program broadcast to teens nationwide.

1958
The National Aeronautics and Space Administration (NASA) opens its doors.

1959
Vice President Richard Nixon and Soviet Premier Nikita Khrushchev engage in their famous "kitchen debate" at the American National Exhibition in Moscow.

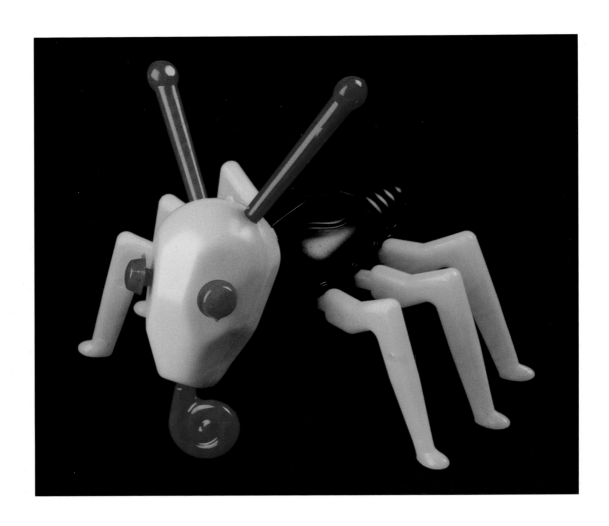

The Game of Cootie
W. H. Schaper Manufacturing Company, Inc.
1966

The Game of Cootie

On March 20, 1950, William Herbert ("Herb") Schaper filed a patent for "a separable toy figure for a construction game." The toy figure, modeled on a wooden fishing lure Schaper (pronounced *shopper*) had whittled in his spare time, was a slightly sinister-looking bug with six legs, two antennae, and a coiled proboscis. It was the kind of creepy-cute toy that appeals to kids—not truly frightening, but just strange enough to elicit a shake of the head or a raised eyebrow from a bemused adult. Schaper knew his audience well. Sidelined during World War II by a ruptured eardrum, he spent his spare time carving and painting wooden animals that he gave to children who visited the Minneapolis store he operated. "He was the greatest man in the world, the kindest human being I ever met," recalled his stepson, Bob Heiber. "I was 16 years old when I came into his life—no youngster—but he treated me with such compassion. He listened."

By the time Schaper filed his patent, games featuring his remarkable insect were being sold on consignment at Dayton's, a Minneapolis department store. The Game of Cootie, as Schaper named it, was marching right off the shelves and into kids' homes. Dayton's sold more than five thousand games by the end of 1950; two years later, Schaper's company had sold more than a million nationwide.

Herb Schaper's wasn't the first game featuring the infamous little creature known as a "cootie," a name invented by World War I soldiers who endured lice-infested trenches. Several Cootie games were in circulation after the war, most notably a 1939 offering by Transogram featuring a three-dimensional wooden bug assembled in a tray. Was Schaper aware of these games? It's certainly a possibility. But he took the concept in a different direction, using the newly available technology of injection molding to create a brightly colored, three-dimensional plastic

"

Even after he carved that little bug, I don't think Herb realized what he had

You don't know the research that went into designing Cootie. He wanted a rough-looking bug like the cooties from the First World War. He knew the kids would embrace it.

I think about his long journey, how he did so many odd jobs—including carrying the mail and working on a highway in Alaska—before I married him, and how Cootie changed his life. Even after he carved that little bug, I don't think Herb realized what he had.

People tell me that he was a man before his time. But any child who has ever played with Cootie knows that Herb came at just the perfect time.
FRAN SCHAPER, Herb's wife

The Cootie Company

bug that was like nothing kids had seen before. Schaper took advantage of another emerging technology to move his toy off the shelves, too—he was one of the first toy makers to recognize the power of television advertising, and he purchased spots on the *Captain Kangaroo* show.

From humble beginnings, Cootie has risen to unforeseen heights. A giant version floated in the 1975 Macy's Thanksgiving Day Parade, and in 2003 the Toy Industry Association included Cootie in its "Century of Toys" list. Cootie is made by Hasbro these days, and Schaper's angular, somewhat menacing little creation has been replaced by a benign, chubby bug with a goofy grin. But the name has remained, and with it, the memory of a Minneapolis man who loved kids and knew what they wanted.

Herb Schaper with the Game of Cootie, 1950s

18

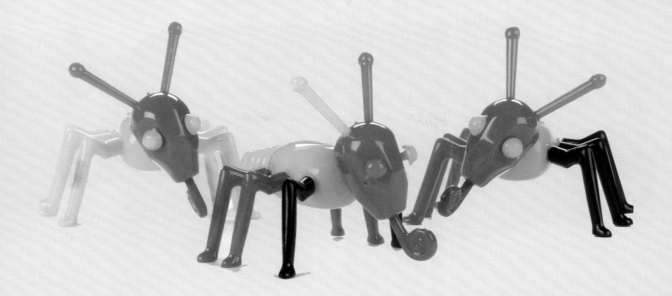

"

It's where I learned the word "proboscis"

I played with my Grandma Green at her kitchen table in Park River, North Dakota. She had an old-time set from the '50s or '60s, and I always wanted the pink body and told her she should have the green body. It was fun to roll the dice and put our cooties together, "no cheating."

And one other thing about Cootie—it's where I learned the word "proboscis," which tickled me because it sounds so funny. My grandma would find reasons to call my nose my "proboscis" to make me laugh.

CARISSA GREEN, b. 1972, administrative secretary

Carissa Green holding her sister, Megan

American Flyer S Gauge Trains

A. C. Gilbert Company

1952–62

American Flyer Trains

"There's something about a train that's magic." So goes the jingle used by Amtrak in the 1980s and '90s to promote the splendor of rail travel. That magic plays out in toys, as well. The fascination with model railroading has lasted nearly as long as there have been locomotives. Miniature railroad collecting began in the 1830s in Europe, where master tinsmiths handcrafted elaborately decorated models, some of which operated with clockwork mechanisms. Model trains gained a foothold in America in the 1850s with mass-produced cars made of heavy-gauge tin, and by the beginning of the twentieth century, several of America's most beloved toy train makers had established themselves, including Ives, Lionel, and American Flyer.

American Flyer began in 1907 as the Edmonds-Metzel Manufacturing Company, a Chicago-based hardware manufacturing business that made tinplate wind-up trains. The line became immensely popular, and in 1910 the company changed its name to the American Flyer Manufacturing Company. In 1938 American Flyer was purchased by Alfred Carlton Gilbert, a Connecticut toy maker who had achieved phenomenal success in 1913 as the inventor of the Erector set. Gilbert continued to

American Flyer Trains
ERECTOR AND OTHER GILBERT TOYS

My wish was for a train

Back in the early '50s, we did not have excess money, but my parents were overly generous to us at Christmas. They scrimped and saved the rest of the year. At Christmas, we were allowed one present that "if it is the only present you received for the rest of your life . . . what would it be?" My wish was for a train.
RICHARD KLICK,
b. 1942, truck sales manager

manufacture American Flyer's signature O gauge electric trains until World War II, when the company diverted its operations to help with the war effort.

In a stroke of marketing savvy, Gilbert discontinued Flyer's O gauge train line in 1946 and replaced it with the two-rail S gauge system—its track providing a sense of realism that the three-track system of competitors Lionel and Marx couldn't match. Train production peaked in the mid-1950s, a time characterized by the creation of some of the most colorful and sought-after American Flyer items. By the early 1960s, however, toy trains began to decline in popularity, mirroring a downturn in rail travel—the result of increased automobile ownership and a dramatic rise in passenger air travel. Consumers were buying toys at discount retailers rather than traditional toy stores and department stores, and their emphasis had shifted away from high-quality, lasting products toward fad items that were less expensive to produce. When Alfred C. Gilbert died in 1961, his son, Alfred Jr., took over the business and subsequently sold a controlling interest to the Wrather Group. By 1966, American Flyer was sold to Lionel, which continues to produce popular American Flyer pieces.

Richard Klick standing at left

To A Man about to Buy an Electric Train for His Boy: A 1954 message from A. C. Gilbert

The train you purchase now is the heart of your boy's own railroad line, the equipment he will work and play with for a long time. That's why you should consider carefully the merits of each brand and decide which one will give him what he is looking for—a toy train or a real railroad. For there is a big difference between one electric train and another. **DO YOU WANT RE-ALISM?** Several years ago all electric trains ran on three-rail track with the current carried in a third rail running down the middle. All trains but American Flyer still use that system. But no one ever saw a real railroad with a track in the middle, so in 1940 we changed to two-rail track. We knew from experience that boys want trains which are accurate copies of the real thing, not trains which no one ever saw in every-day life . . . Big-gauge trains cannot be made to scale because they would be too large for the average home or apartment and would be far too expensive for most people to buy. We didn't like this stumpy, squat look in electric trains so we selected a new gauge which would permit us to make true scale models. This gauge is called "S," which was midway between "HO" (too small for youngsters) and "O" (too big to make scale models) . . . Our trains in their new scale and on their two-rail track were scaled down versions of the kind seen on America's big railroads. American Flyer trains have been used in miniature movie sets and on TV shows to represent real trains moving across the countryside. No other make of electric trains could have possibly been used in this way.

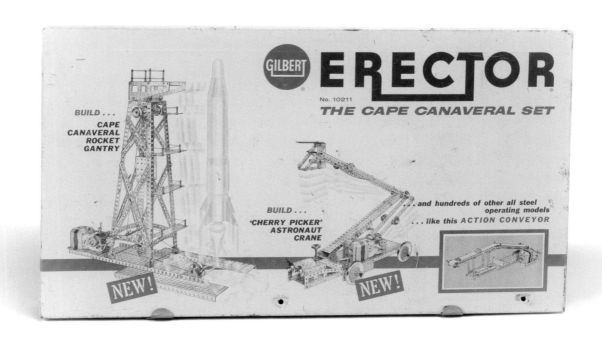

Cape Canaveral Erector Set

A. C. Gilbert Company

1962

Erector Set

When it comes to toys, the words "some assembly required" aren't often welcomed by parents. But every once in a while, a toy comes along where assembly is the sole purpose, a task left to the child that engages the imaginative mind while providing countless hours of fun. And for almost a hundred years, Erector sets have done just that, becoming one of the most iconic building toys of all time. Possibly the longest-lasting successful toy in American history, the Erector was conceived during a commuter train ride. Alfred Carlton Gilbert, a magician and the maker of Mysto toys, dreamed up the idea in 1911 while traveling from his home in New Haven, Connecticut, to New York City. From his train window, Gilbert watched workers building a power-line tower. Later that day, Gilbert went home and began fashioning beams and girders out of corrugated cardboard for a miniature construction set that would match the steel beams the workers were using. The next day he had Mysto's workers duplicate the prototype in tin.

Introduced to the public in 1913 as the "Mysto Erector Structural Steel Builder," the kit featured evenly spaced holes for bolts to pass through, and screws, bolts, pulleys, and gears similar to those employed in real construction. The set was also backed by the first major American ad campaign for a toy, marketed with the catchphrase, "Hello Boys, Make Lots of Toys." (Girls wouldn't be featured—much less mentioned—in advertising campaigns for the Erector until the 1940s.) The Erector quickly became a hit, allowing kids to build everything from skyscrapers, bridges, and railways to powered windmills, vehicles, and elevators. Gilbert responded to demand by releasing more and more elaborate sets. Perhaps the greatest period for the Erector was between 1924 and 1932, when specific models, such as the steam shovel, White Truck, Ferris wheel, Zeppelin, and Hudson locomotive and tender were released.

" The possibilities were endless

The legacy of the Erector is undeniable as a toy which, through creative play, inspired several generations of children to become architects, engineers, and scientists. But the toy also inspired grown-up innovators. In 1940 Donald Bailey of Britain's Royal Engineers used his childhood Erector set to design the portable Bailey bridge, which spanned creeks and rivers and was hailed by General Dwight D. Eisenhower as one of the three most important technological advancements of World War II. In 1950 Yale Medical School students William Sewell Jr. and William W. L. Glenn used Erector set pieces to create a heart pump for experimental bypass surgery on dogs, and in 1961 Czech chemist Otto Wichterle employed the motor of an old phonograph and a child's Erector set to discover the spin-casting process used in manufacturing soft contact lenses. Nobel Prize–winning physicist and former U.S. Secretary of Energy Dr. Steven Chu was also inspired by the Erector at an early age. In his 1997 Nobel autobiography Dr. Chu recalled,

In the summer after kindergarten, a friend introduced me to the joys of building plastic model airplanes and warships. By the fourth grade, I graduated to an Erector set and spent many happy hours constructing devices of unknown purpose where the main design criterion was to maximize the number of moving parts and overall size. The living room rug was frequently littered with hundreds of metal "girders" and tiny nuts and bolts surrounding half-finished structures. An understanding mother allowed me to keep the projects going for days on end.
DR. STEVEN CHU, b. 1948, scientist

Build yourself a great kid.

Here is a complete list of ingredients:
1 average boy interested in average things—used to playing with average toys.
1 Erector Set.
You supply ingredient #1. We've been supplying #2 for over 50 years.
Our business is teaching kids how to enjoy time—not how to kill it.

And we have seen the look in thousands of kids' faces when they made their first steel bridge or The Empire State Building or whatever their imaginative minds conceived.
We think every kid ought to have the chance to have that look in his eyes.

Erector Sets
build great kids.

Gilbert Division of Gabriel Industries, Inc.

16

After World War II, the growth of the baby boom brought strong sales for several years. The most ambitious set, introduced in 1948, came with multiple electric motors that could be used to build a walking robot. But Erector's popularity began to decline as early as 1950. Not one new edition was added for eight years, and the company failed to modernize the available models. Besides a decline in innovation, competition from other products such as Tinker Toys, Lincoln Logs, and LEGOs took a toll. By the late 1950s, A. C. Gilbert Sr. had turned the company over to his son, A. C. Gilbert Jr. The company went out of business in 1967, the year the last Erector sets were produced at the original factory.

View-Master

Sawyer's, Inc.

1959–77

View-Master

It could take you to exotic places past, present, and future—real or imagined—and all in dynamic, full-color 3-D. The View-Master grew out of our fascination with the stereoscope, a popular parlor pastime of the nineteenth century that made photographic prints appear to come alive. The device held a stereograph card containing two slightly different images of the same scene which, when viewed through the twin lenses of the stereoscope, simulated binocular depth perception. From the carnage of Civil War battlefields to the pyramids of Egypt, the stereoscope brought it all into the home in graphic, dimensional detail.

Photographers continued to tinker with the stereographic process for decades in an effort to make the experience even more spectacular. In 1938 camera buff William Gruber was experimenting with a new technique: he tied two cameras together and then transferred the prints to Kodachrome color transparency film. The images were then mounted on a reel and viewed using a simple hand-operated viewer. Gruber was photographing at Oregon Caves National Monument when his innovative process caught the eye of postcard publisher Harold Graves. Gruber agreed to join Graves's firm, Sawyer's, Inc., and in 1939 the View-Master debuted at the New York World's Fair.

The first generations of reels contained seven images and were sold individually. The subjects, much like their nineteenth-century stereograph predecessors, were primarily scenic views and education sets depicting everything from wildflower species to stories from the Bible. During World War II the company produced millions of reels for the U.S. military to aid with artillery spotting and aircraft recognition training. In 1951 Sawyer's purchased rival company Tru-Vue, which held a license with Walt Disney Studios. Sawyer's now had a veritable gold mine of Disney characters, television programs, and theme park oppor-

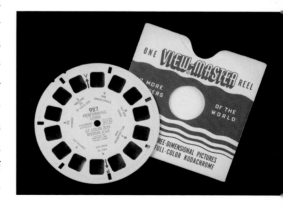

tunities for their reels. Sales exploded, compelling the company to shift its emphasis from travelogue subjects to entertainment themes. View-Master had found a new audience, and the device initially intended as an educational tool for adults was now a toy—much to the delight of children everywhere.

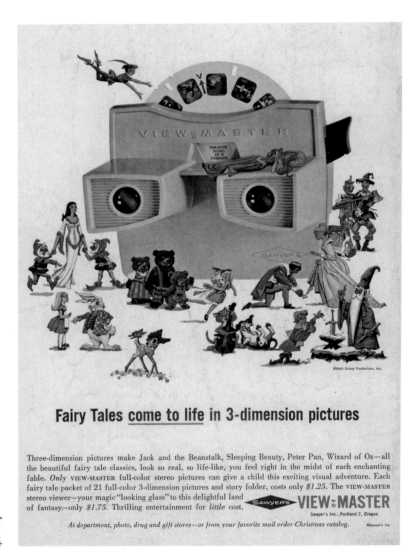

Fairy Tales come to life in 3-dimension pictures

Three-dimension pictures make Jack and the Beanstalk, Sleeping Beauty, Peter Pan, Wizard of Oz—all the beautiful fairy tale classics, look so real, so life-like, you feel right in the midst of each enchanting fable. *Only* VIEW-MASTER full-color stereo pictures can give a child this exciting visual adventure. Each fairy tale packet of 21 full-color 3-dimension pictures and story folder, costs only *$1.25.* The VIEW-MASTER stereo viewer—your magic "looking glass" to this delightful land of fantasy—only *$1.75.* Thrilling entertainment for *little* cost. SAWYER'S **VIEW-MASTER** Sawyer's Inc., Portland 7, Oregon

At department, photo, drug and gift stores—or from your favorite mail order Christmas catalog. ©Sawyer's Inc.

View-Master advertisement, 1964

Karen Vaughan Kendall, seated, and sister Kitty

"

Like I was actually in the places pictured . . .

When we visited our grand-parents, we always played with an older early version of a 3-D photo viewer. We told stories on when we were going to visit these places "on vacation." Our parents saw this and decided to buy us a View-Master for Christmas. We of course had the Disney films and enjoyed them. Sometimes we made up our own stories as we viewed and talked about the films to the other siblings waiting for their turn. It was a toy that the three of us kids "shared."

I still remember the phrase "My Turn" as we played with the View-Master!

RICHARD KLICK, b. 1942, truck sales manager

I loved my View-Master! Mine was dark brown. Pointing it at the window to get extra light made me feel like I was actually in the places pictured. I only had a couple of disks, so I got to know the photos pretty well. I think they were of Yellowstone. I remember having to take really good care to keep the View-Master out of my little sister's reach. She kept wanting to poke the pictures out of the disks. I'm sure my parents were subject to excessive shrieking about it from both of us!

KAREN VAUGHAN KENDALL, b. 1954, volunteer program associate

Betsy McCall Paper Dolls

1962–64

Betsy McCall Paper Dolls

When the 1950s dawned, the American toy industry was on the cusp of change. With shortages resulting from the Great Depression and World War II receding into memory, toy makers pitched an increasing assortment of "must-have" products to young parents. As the decade unfolded, a dizzying assortment of playthings became available and accessible to children.

But in this world of increasing abundance, there were quiet moments, too. Moments when the combination of pages torn from magazines, a pair of scissors, and a vivid imagination were enough to keep a child enchanted for hours. Betsy McCall, the sweet-faced paper doll introduced by *McCall's* magazine in May 1951, came equipped with fashionable clothes, accessories, and a pet dachshund, Nosy. Children could reenact the stories told by *McCall's* each month, but they could also take off on their own paths, placing their ever-expanding ranks of Betsy and her friends into situations of their own choosing. The May 1960 issue featured Betsy's trip down the Mississippi—but who's to say that Betsy's plaid shirt and clamdiggers weren't also the perfect garb for scaling a mountain built from pillows and bedspreads?

The long history of paper dolls published in women's magazines stretches back at least to 1859, when *Godey's Lady's Book* printed a black-and-white doll with costumes for children to color. Beginning in the early twentieth century, *Ladies' Home Journal, Good Housekeeping,* and many other magazines including *McCall's* published paper dolls. Dainty blonde Lettie Lane, the paper doll featured in *Ladies' Home Journal* from 1908 to 1915, was representative of her era. Each month a full page was given over to Lettie, her friends, family members, and their servants, all of whom were detailed in color by Sheila Young, a well-known magazine illustrator. A story accompanied each month's collection of dolls and clothing, which were intended to

be cut out and mounted on heavy paper or cardboard for durability. In 1912 the magazine capitalized on Lettie's popularity. A cardboard dollhouse, complete with furniture and a small bisque figure, was offered as "The Wonderful New Bungalow Home of a Most Delightful Little Lady." And how did eager young readers attain this treasure? The magazine editors explained: "Send to us THREE new yearly subscriptions for THE LADIES' HOME JOURNAL, accompanied by the regular subscription price ($4.50 for the three) . . . whereupon the house, furniture and doll will be sent, all shipping expenses prepaid."

In the midst of the Great Depression, paper dolls became popular gifts for children whose families could afford little else. These stand-alone sets, often modeled on celebrities like Shirley Temple, remained in vogue into the 1950s, when TV stars like Annette Funicello and Patty Duke were celebrated in miniature, two-dimensional form.

Betsy McCall stood apart from her celebrity counterparts. She was an ordinary little girl with an admittedly enviable wardrobe. Her monthly adventures—from trimming the tree to going on a picnic to visiting Washington, DC—fueled the imaginations of children, mostly girls. For while male dolls were occasionally included, and boys certainly played with Betsy, her story was first and foremost written for girls. She was a well-clad, impeccably groomed role model who enjoyed a life combining leisure, learning, and community service. She offered girls the same form of inspiration that the other features in *McCall's* offered the grown women in their lives. Think of it as a fine example of parallel play—each month, *McCall's* gave women of all ages the chance to dream, to imagine, to be carried away to a brand-new world of their own making.

Here's Betsy McCall!

So neat...so sweet... with dainty features molded of BAKELITE Vinyl Resins

Winsome, well-dressed Betsy is perfection to the last detail. Her sweet face, as soft and washable as any little girl's, won't crack, break, scuff or peel...thanks to the special qualities of BAKELITE Vinyl Resins.

Adorable dolls, like this Ideal creation, are just one of countless ways these versatile plastics add to your life—from floorings that seal out dirt to dish drainers that don't get gummy. Both industry and defense find dependable BAKELITE Vinyl Resins always meet their high standards. *You* can count on the BAKELITE trademark in all *you* buy.

The official Betsy McCall doll, beautifully dressed in one of Betsy's favorite dresses. Millions of children follow her adventures monthly in McCall's magazine. A McCall pattern is included for adding to her wardrobe ...other patterns available. And her shining hair can be combed and curled with her own curlers of BAKELITE Vinyl Resins. Made by Ideal Toy Corporation, Hollis 7, N.Y.

BAKELITE
TRADE-MARK
VINYL RESINS

TRADE Ⓑ MARK

BAKELITE COMPANY
A Division of Union Carbide and Carbon Corporation UCC 30 East 42nd St., New York 17, N.

Betsy's page was all mine

I fondly remember Betsy McCall paper dolls. My grandmother subscribed to McCall's magazine and I anxiously awaited its arrival each month. Betsy's page was all mine and I carefully cut out the page, then cut out the Betsy doll and her new wardrobe. I developed creativity and artistically by tracing the doll on plain paper and designing and drawing more clothes for her. My friends and I often used them as puppet characters in plays in our shoebox puppet theater.

DIANNE BECKER HOON, b. 1947, mom, grandma, and native of St. Paul, Minnesota

Sweet Sue
American Character Doll Company
1953

Sweet Sue

She wasn't much for cuddling. In fact, with her carefully coiffed hair and designer wardrobe, she was the kind of doll that even her youngest admirers knew to keep at arm's length. And yet, her standoffish personality didn't keep her from being one of the most popular dolls of the 1950s.

American Character made a number of best-selling dolls over the years, from the realistic Tiny Tears baby doll of the early 1950s to a version of "Little Ricky" from the *I Love Lucy* television show to Tressy, a teen doll that debuted in 1964. But Sweet Sue—"the most glamorous doll in the world," according to the brochure packaged with her—was something special. She could be dressed in a wide array of outfits, including smart, fashion-forward pleated skirts and starched shirts, silk ball gowns, and lacy chiffon peignoir sets. Her hard plastic body was a reflection of her somewhat rigid demeanor, yet she was surprisingly flexible. She could bend at the waist, knees, and elbows, assume a variety of poses, and clasp her hands. Later versions could even walk a bit. And of course, her penetrating eyes could blink or even wink, should such a coy movement be deemed acceptable.

Sweet Sue was sold in five sizes over the years, from fourteen inches tall to a thirty-one-inch "life-sized" model. Her crowning glory was her hair, which could be styled and accented with a variety of accessories coordinated with her outfits.

Sweet Sue was a true "fashion doll," designed for children who enjoyed dressing her in the types of

> ## December 25, 1955
> *My brother was behind my mother [as she took the picture], taking aim at those dolls with his new Christmas bow and arrow. He hated our dolls. Later, he took the dolls outside and leaned them against a cottonwood tree. He put an apple on their heads for target practice. He missed the apple and hit the dolls!*
> YVONNE (DUGAS) JOHNSON, b. 1951, electrical assembler

Yvonne Dugas, right, with sister Cheryl

37

clothing they aspired to wear in their adult years. She was one of several dolls of her era who paved the way for Barbie, the ultimate fashionista. The doll for preteens and teenagers who were emerging from childhood into the exciting, uncertain world of young adulthood, Sweet Sue invited role-playing—a chance to try on grown-up personalities while engaging in the familiar world of doll play. She may not have been the doll you looked for when you needed a hug. But her association with those bittersweet teen years makes her the doll you want to hold on to forever.

"This doll began my doll-collecting journey

In December of 1953, having just turned six in October, I was diagnosed with scarlet fever. This meant missing out on all of the Christmas holiday activities at school and at church. However, Santa Claus brought me the most beautiful doll that I had ever seen. She was twenty-four inches tall, a "Sweet Sue," and I was in awe! Mom taught me how to take good care of her and her beautiful clothes. To this day, I believe that this doll began my doll-collecting journey.

JANET PETERSON LEE, b. 1947, office manager

Raggedy Ann and Andy
Handmade by Eleanor Schwartau Annexstad
1952

Raggedy Ann and Andy

Whatever the size, shape, or material, a doll can serve as an extension of a child, providing comfort and companionship. For centuries, all dolls—like everything else—were handmade and one of a kind. Mass production of dolls began in Germany in the early 1800s, when thousands of papier-mâché doll heads were made from a single mold. Since then, of course, the manufacturing of dolls has spread worldwide, with each doll a reflection of the availability and workability of materials and, most importantly, changing tastes.

Yet there's something about a handmade doll—the simplicity, the warmth, the sense of nostalgia—that makes it a perennial favorite of children and adults. And nowhere is this sense of nostalgia more apparent than in the age-old appeal of Raggedy Ann and Andy dolls.

The story of Raggedy Ann and Andy is the stuff of legend. It is often told like this: Young Marcella Delight Gruelle found a battered rag doll in her attic. She brought it to her father, *New York Herald* cartoonist Johnny Gruelle, who drew a face on the old doll. Marcella played with the doll constantly, and soon a rag doll named "Rags" was showing up in *Mr. Twee Deedle,* Gruelle's comic strip about a small sprite who dispensed life lessons on honesty, thoughtfulness, and other virtues. In 1915 Gruelle received a design patent on a doll based on Rags. Later that year, Marcella Gruelle died at the age of thirteen after receiving a controversial smallpox vaccination. It is said that after her death, her father kept the rag doll close by as a remembrance of his daughter. In 1918 Johnny Gruelle published *Raggedy Ann Stories*. A sequel, *Raggedy Andy Stories,* followed in 1920.

The first Raggedy Ann dolls also appeared in 1918. The original dolls were handmade, with individually painted and stitched facial features. Instant hits, they were soon being

What joy and happiness you have brought into this world!

For *Raggedy Ann Stories*, cartoonist Johnny Gruelle wrote a poignant dedication that hinted at his history of love and loss: *As I write this, I have before me on my desk, propped up against the telephone, an old rag doll . . . what joy and happiness you have brought into this world! And no matter what treatment you have received, how patient you have been! . . . So, to the millions of children and grownups who have loved a Rag Doll, I dedicate these stories of Raggedy Ann.*

mass-produced. Over the decades many companies have held licenses to produce Raggedy Ann and Andy, including Knickerbocker Toy Company and Hasbro/Playskool. But patterns for making homemade versions of these ever-popular dolls with their wide, happy grins and permanently outstretched arms have sold as well if not better than their manufactured counterparts. No matter how much the world changes, no matter how many new products are introduced, it seems the appeal of a doll created by hand for a special child will never disappear.

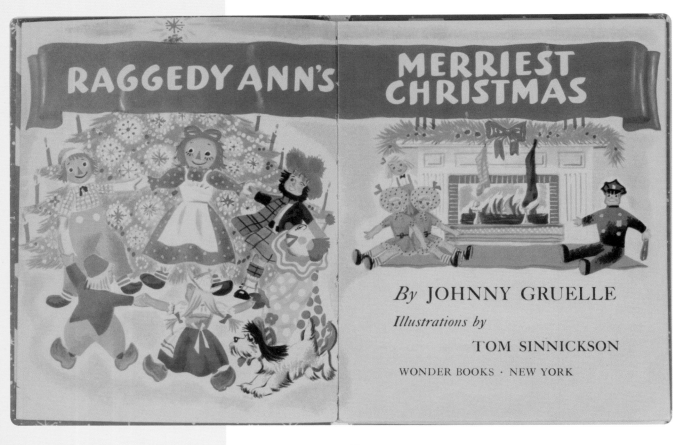

RAGGEDY ANN'S MERRIEST CHRISTMAS

By JOHNNY GRUELLE

Illustrations by

TOM SINNICKSON

WONDER BOOKS · NEW YORK

> ## "They were cuddly and comforting to me all through my childhood

My mother, Eleanor Schwartau Annexstad, was a gifted seamstress. When I was a very little girl, she presented me with Raggedy Ann and Raggedy Andy—dolls that she sewed on her 1949 White sewing machine. They were cuddly and comforting to me all through my childhood. My mother read to me the stories of Raggedy Ann and Andy— stories of kindness and helpfulness to others. We read them at nap time, or over cups of pretend tea. Of course Raggedy Ann and Andy were propped up at the table listening, too.

For my fourteenth birthday, my mother sewed a new Raggedy Ann, who eventually saw me through the traumas of high school and especially during mother's illness and death from cancer when I was sixteen. That Raggedy Ann went with me to college.

KAREN ANNEXSTAD HUMPHREY, b. 1950, grateful daughter, wife, mother

Ike-A-Doo Krazy Ikes Game
Whitman Publishing Company
1954

Ike-A-Doo

Krazy Ikes were first introduced as a wooden construction toy in the 1920s. A cross between Tinker Toys and jointed dolls, Krazy Ikes were sold in sets of parts that could be assembled into people, animals, and more: "a thousand funny things, all different," according to the toys' maker, Knapp Electric Company of Indianapolis. Bodies, heads, and feet were held together by pencil-thin dowels. Once completed, the figures could assume all sorts of crazy positions.

Due to material shortages and conversion of factories to war use, many popular toys suspended production during World War II, but not Krazy Ikes. Because there were no rationing restrictions on wood, they remained available throughout the war.

If you have fond memories of endless hours spent assembling fabulous Krazy Ike creations, you might be a little confused right now. "I remember all those little parts," you're thinking to yourself, "but weren't they plastic?" In the 1950s Whitman Publishing Company (best known for its varied line of children's books) purchased the rights to Krazy Ikes. In the postwar years, the new material of choice for toy manufacturers was plastic. The earliest plastics on the market were brittle and even flammable, but they were soon replaced by higher-quality products that held their color and were washable, light, durable, and economical to produce. This is the world described by historian Jeffrey Meikle (*American Plastic: A Cultural History,* 1995):

> American boys abandoned labor-intensive balsa-wood model-building in favor of mass-produced kits by Revell and Aurora with injection-molded polystyrene parts easily twisted from connecting sprues and glued together following step-by-step instructions. Plastic cars, ships, and fighter planes, their

intricate realistic details a product of mold-making rather than model-making, seemed to take pride of place in the bedroom of every pre-teen male.

Krazy Ikes marched into the modern age without missing a beat.

Perhaps taking a cue from perennial top-seller the Game of Cootie, Whitman moved beyond selling sets of plastic parts and developed the Ike-A-Doo game, in which players raced to be the first to complete a figure. Players were assigned one of four Krazy Ike figures: Dopey-Ike, Ike-A-Roo, Cap'n-Ike, and the perpetually seated Lazy-Ike. As players took turns spinning for parts, play continued until the winner yelled, "IKE-A-DOO!" And like Cootie, if players tired of competing, they could amuse themselves constructing the cheerful little figures. With a game like this, you can't lose.

I found them a little creepy

I played with Krazy Ikes, but I found them a little creepy. What was that long-snouted yellow head, anyway: a horse? a dog? a dragon? And what did they have to do with President Eisenhower?

CHERI REGISTER, b. 1945, writer

**Matchbox E-Type Jaguar
and Hot Wheels Custom Camaro**

Lesney Products and Mattel, Inc.
1962–68

Matchbox and Hot Wheels

Matchbox had its beginnings in post–World War II London, where friends Leslie and Rodney Smith established a die-casting business named Lesney Products in 1947. Their first toy offerings were construction vehicles, including a bulldozer, tractor, and cement mixer. In 1953 Lesney engineer Jack Odell made a three-inch-long steamroller for his daughter to take to school. It had to be small enough to fit inside a box of matches—the school's criterion for bringing items from home. The diminutive toy inspired a new product line, and the Matchbox brand was launched.

Early Matchbox offerings repeated the construction theme, but with increasing sales came diversification, and in 1954 Lesney introduced the red-painted double-decked London Bus,

which became one of Matchbox's most iconic vehicles. The company branched out further in 1956 with the Models of Yesteryear line, featuring detailed renditions of vintage cars and buses. The Yesteryear line expanded over the years to include luxury vehicles with enhancements like plastic windows and detailed interiors—now virtually any kid could own a Rolls-Royce, Jaguar, or Mercedes-Benz! By the mid-1960s, Matchbox was becoming a leader in the die-cast car industry.

But when American rival Mattel introduced its Hot Wheels line in 1968, everything changed. Mattel founder Elliot Handler, the driving force behind Hot Wheels, sought to compete with Matchbox by creating vehicles inspired by muscle car drag racing, which had become immensely popular in America in the 1960s. Mattel further solidified its niche by reproducing uniquely American models designed for speed, like the Firebird, Camaro, and Barracuda. Hot Wheels were a smash hit and by 1969 had become the most purchased die-cast cars in the world. A full-fledged drag race was now underway between Matchbox and Hot Wheels.

Taking a page from the Hot Wheels playbook, Matchbox retooled its line with new styling, brighter paint, and a sprightlier wheel design dubbed "Superfast." Matchbox cars continued to sell well and be very popular throughout the 1970s and '80s but couldn't keep up with the dynamic appeal of Hot Wheels. The company was sold in 1992 to Tyco, which was bought out by Mattel in 1997.

From 1968 to 1971, Hot Wheels "redline" cars (named after their red-trimmed tires) came with collector buttons, which have become nearly as popular with collectors as the cars.

MATTEL
HOT WHEELS
MASERATI MISTRAL
©1969 Mattel Inc. Hong Kong

Jane Leonard and sister
Karin with Lassie

You are what you drive . . .

Matchbox or Hot Wheels? Many of us fell into one camp or the other. Matchbox appealed to those who admired traditional, understated cars and realistic detailing. Matchbox cars were made more for looks than for performance. Hot Wheels fans loved the funky body designs and flashy paint jobs, and they had a need for speed. The characters of these competing toy lines mirrored both the origins of their makers and the personalities of the kids who played with them.

As a young child, I played for hours with rubber and plastic cars and pressed-steel Tonka trucks. I soon moved onto Matchbox and Corgi toys. Then came Hot Wheels cars. I still remember my first: a green custom T-Bird from 1968. I was so proud that I carried it with me to Sunday school. I loved the customized muscle cars and the early fantasy vehicles that no other company was creating. But by the sixth grade, I started to miss the realism that Matchbox and other brands such as Husky and Impy perfected in the 1960s. Already—even at twelve—I was nostalgic for the toy cars of my early childhood.

MAC RAGAN, b. 1962, author of *Hot Wheels Cars*

I began collecting Matchbox cars when I was probably six or seven, purchasing a box when my mom took my twin sister and me shopping with her at a big department store. At the time the cars cost forty-four cents which I could pay for out of a weekly allowance of fifty cents. I liked them for several reasons: my mom loved England and they were made there, and that made them somehow exotic. Each conjured up a story—like the Land Rover and how I saw the same vehicle in the movie Hatari. I loved the boxes. I loved how sturdy and realistic the cars and trucks were . . . especially how the doors and hoods and trunks opened, and the vehicles that carried things (dogs, horses, cattle, pipes, scaffolding, etc.) came with those things. One of my favorites is the Studebaker station wagon, because it came with a sliding top, hunter, and hunting dog, and reminded me of my outdoorsman grandpa, whom I adored.

JANE LEONARD, b. 1957, community and leadership development professional

Davy Crockett Coonskin Cap
George S. Bailey Hat Company
or Weathermac Corporation
1955

Davy Crockett Coonskin Cap

First, the facts: David (his preferred name) Crockett probably didn't wear one. The first rendering of the celebrated frontiersman in a coonskin cap appeared in 1837, a year after his death, on the cover of the *Davy Crockett Almanac*. While fur caps were stylish on the frontier, it's most likely that the wildcat-skin-cap-wearing Nimrod Wildfire—a character created in 1831 based on Crockett—was the origin of the coonskin cap legend, which stuck like proverbial glue.

Fast forward to the early 1950s, when Walt Disney signs a tall, lanky Texan named Fess Parker to star as David Crockett in an upcoming series for the *Disneyland* television show. Heralded as the first TV miniseries, the trilogy of episodes—"Davy Crockett: Indian Fighter," "Davy Crockett Goes to Congress," and "Davy Crockett at the Alamo"—aired during the winter of 1954–55 to great popular acclaim. Disney's Crockett perpetuated the nineteenth-century incarnation of Davy as an icon of romantic melodrama—more myth than man—at a time when post–World War II America was hungry for heroes. And it's not hard to understand why, as television viewers were still reeling from the infused paranoia whipped up by broadcasts of Senator Joseph McCarthy's communist witch-hunt earlier that year. Cast against a media-made world of "us against them," the age-old fable of good versus evil was played out to perfection by Disney's gutsy and patriotic Davy.

Parker's signature appearance, including buckskin jacket, Kentucky rifle, and, of course, coonskin cap, set off a tidal wave of merchandising—with baby boomer boys in the marketing crosshairs. There were Davy Crockett plastic frontier fringe costumes, toy muskets and powder horns, trading cards, board

games, puzzles, coloring books, and lunchboxes. But of the three thousand items produced in 1955 to satisfy the public's thirst for all things Crockett, nothing was more popular than the coonskin cap. More than five thousand of the faux fur caps were sold per day during the height of the fad. Kids put them on when they woke up and didn't take them off until they went to bed—and sometimes not even then! There was even a white faux fur variation made for girls called the Polly Crockett. Although Parker's character—like the real David Crockett—died at the Alamo in episode three, he was resurrected for the 1955–56 season due to popular demand. But Crockett mania began to wane by early 1956, as audiences became engaged with other TV characters. Ironically, Fess Parker returned to television in the early 1960s as the legendary frontier hero Daniel Boone, again sporting a coonskin cap (which, unfortunately, Boone didn't wear either).

"Everybody in my class but me was Davy Crockett

Remember when Davy Crockett hit the theaters in 1955? I guess I was in third grade at the time. Suddenly the next day, everybody in my class but me was Davy Crockett. And because I didn't have my coonskin cap and my powder horn, or Old Betsy, my rifle, and the chaps, I was deemed the Mexican leader, Santa Anna.

And everybody came after me with the butt ends of their flintlock rifles. And they chased me home from school until I got my parents to buy me a coonskin cap.

STEVEN SPIELBERG, b. 1946, motion picture director, from *Spielberg Interviews*, 2000

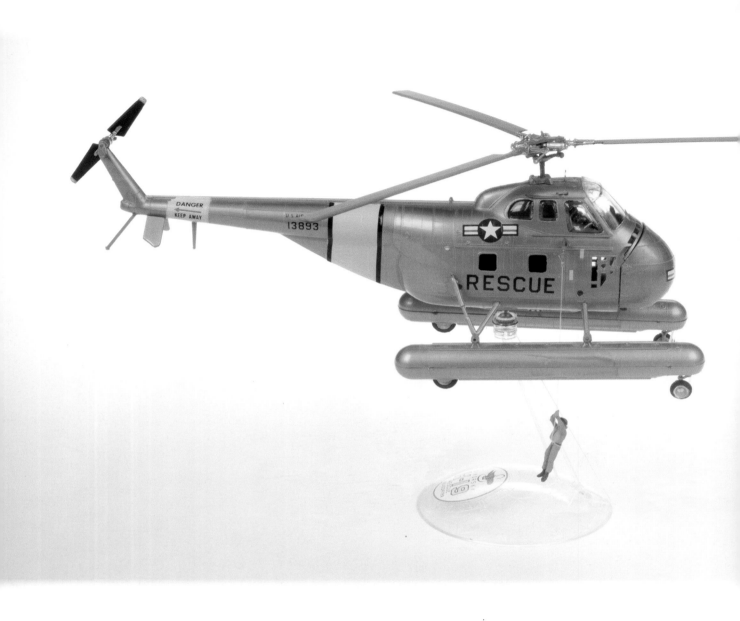

Sikorsky H-19 Rescue Helicopter
Revell Company
1955–78

Revell Model Kits

Planes, trains, and automobiles . . . and tanks, battleships, and spacecraft. If you were building plastic models as a kid during the 1950s, '60s, and '70s, chances are Revell had you covered. Authenticity was the company's forte and the detailing was amazing, so good that in 1960 the Kremlin purchased several kits to beef up Soviet intelligence on U.S. warship designs. But Revell did more than make precise reproductions; it revolutionized the concept of a "buildable" model and helped to make modeling one of the most popular hobbies for young and old alike during the mid-twentieth century.

Revell grew out of a company named Precision Specialties, a plastics firm started in 1941 by California entrepreneur Lewis Glaser. At that time, most model kits were made of wood, but Glaser saw potential in the use of plastics to create accurate, buildable models. In the early 1950s Precision Specialties manufactured the "Highway Pioneers," a plastic car kit series conceived by the British design firm of Gowland and Gowland. The kits were a great success, and in 1953 Glaser's company, now named Revell, launched a model of the battleship USS *Missouri* based on an in-house design. Military kits have always been especially popular with modelers seeking not only to connect with history but to replicate the innovative and creative mechanical designs developed as a result of war. Revell quickly released more kits, including World War II aircraft and warships, jet fighters, sailing ships, and spacecraft—all based on Glaser's philosophy that the models should be historically accurate representations and be easy to build. To achieve those goals, Revell's engineers created meticulous plans based on photographs and other documentation, while sculptors crafted patterns for every part. A prototype had to pass an assembly test before molds were cast.

"Like father, like son . . . and daughter

My father made balsa wood and tissue-paper model airplanes when he was a boy and his enjoyment with the model hobby lasted into adulthood. When plastic model kits became popular during the 1950s, I can remember both of my parents getting involved with this new hobby. This often started by picking up one of the Revell/Gowland Highway Pioneers antique car kits from a local hardware store or paint store which had a display rack showcasing this first very simple model kit series. Eventually,

I started making model kits myself. One of my favorite model kits was Revell's Sikorsky H-19 Rescue Helicopter. This kit originally sold for ninety-eight cents and the photo shows me watching my dad building it in 1958 when I was six years old. Years later, Revell rereleased this helicopter kit in different packaging. I had to build one myself, so in 1995 I did, recreating that same scene with my six-year-old daughter Kelly watching me build it.

GARY HOFMEISTER, b. 1951, workplace safety consultant

Always strong in its inventory of classic car offerings, Revell took advantage of America's infatuation with hot rods and racing by releasing a line of customized kits in the 1960s styled after vehicles designed by renowned hot rodder Ed "Big Daddy" Roth. Roth's unconventional creations—like the bubble-topped "Beatnik Bandit," the twin-engine "Mysterion," and the "Orbitron," which featured red, green, and blue headlamps—offered young modelers an opportunity for rebellious self-expression, much to the consternation of parents. Revell also marketed a series of Roth's hot rod characters, including his famous Mickey Mouse antihero Rat Fink, which became a counterculture icon. Despite its achievements as a pioneer in the precision model industry, Revell fell on hard times during the 1980s as public interest in the hobby waned, and the company was merged with longtime competitor Monogram in 1986.

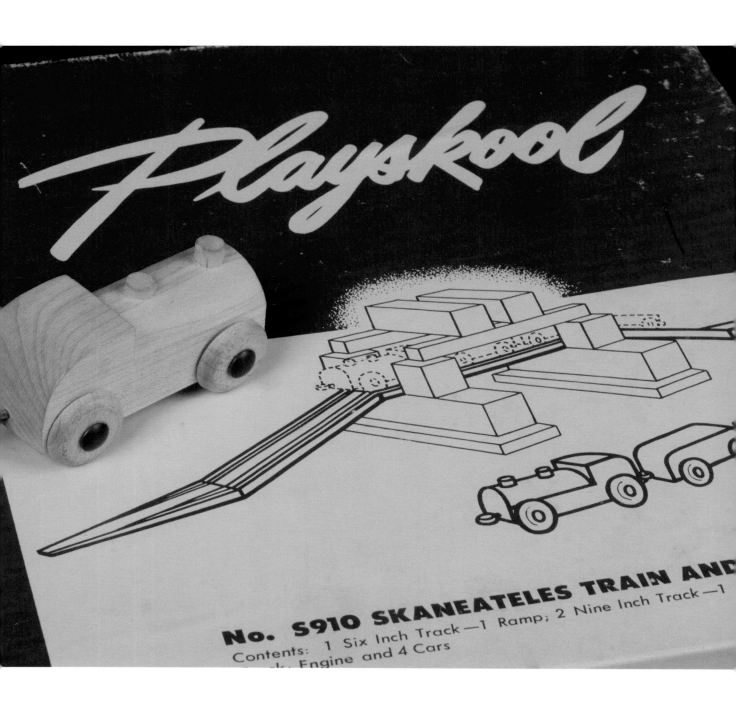

No. S910 SKANEATELES TRAIN AND
Contents: 1 Six Inch Track—1 Ramp; 2 Nine Inch Track—1
Track; Engine and 4 Cars

Skaneateles Train and Track Set
Playskool Manufacturing Company
1956–60s

Skaneateles Train Set

In *Toys and Culture,* play theorist Brian Sutton-Smith makes an insightful, if world-weary, observation: "We have little compelling evidence of a connection between toys, all by themselves, and achievement . . . What is more obvious is that, since the appearance of toys in the seventeenth century, we have steadily and progressively developed a belief that there is a connection between toys and achievement."

In support of Sutton-Smith's assertion, we submit Exhibit A: a simple abstracted train set made of varnished Vermont maple, loaded with the aspirations of postwar parents who believed in the promise of educational toys.

The Playskool Institute was founded in 1928 as a division of the John Schroeder Lumber Company of Milwaukee, Wisconsin. The company's early advertising promised "Playthings with a Purpose," as manifested in its first successful offering, a child-sized desk with pegboards and blocks called the Home Kindergarten. The institute (note that it was *not* called a toy company) offered an "extension course" in childrearing to its members (product purchasers).

The idea of training children to be productive adults through imaginative play gained a strong foothold throughout the 1950s and '60s, and Playskool was a major proponent of the philosophy. In addition to serving as the distributor for a line of wooden toys produced by Snear Ithaca, by the end of the 1950s Playskool had acquired the J. L. Wright Company (founded by Frank Lloyd Wright's son and notable for its Lincoln Logs), Halsam Products (known, among other things, for their embossed alphabet blocks), and Holgate Brothers (makers of a popular line of nursery-school toys). The company's sales would continue to rise in the 1960s, due in part to the creation of the federal Head Start school-prep program.

(1)

(Shown above) PLAYSKOOL'S FAMOUS SKANEATELES TRAIN, TRACK AND BLOCK SETS offer hours of imaginative play for children 1 to 9. Beautifully made of durable, natural finish northern hard maple—precision-cut, carefully sanded and waxed. Washable. Tracks fit perfectly with tongue-and-groove construction. Pieces in all sets are interchangeable. Design Sheet included. Accessories (1) to (4) add to play value, make railroad layout more interesting.

DE LUXE 55-PC. SET with Highway Crossing Accessories. 188 inches of track—makes Oval with Figure 8 Crossover layout (and all layouts of smaller sets). Train with engine, 5 cars is abt. 17½ in. long. Four 9-in. straight track, four 6 in.; 12 curved track, 2 fitter tracks, crossover, 4 switches, 2 lead-on ramps; 2 road approaches, crossing sign, gate, semaphore, auto, 2 trucks. 12 assorted blocks.

48 T 606—Ship. wt. 5 lbs. 8 oz........Set $11.69

36-PC. SET. 148 inches of track—makes Figure 8 Crossover layout with Double Switch-out (also makes Straightaway, Serpentine or Circle). Train with engine, 4 cars is abt. 14½ in. long. Six 6-in. straight track, 12 curved track, crossover, 2 switches, 2 lead-on ramps. 8 assorted building blocks.

48 T 605—Ship. wt. 4 lbs..............Set $7.94

22-PC. BASIC SET. 67 inches of track make Circle with Switch-out or Serpentine layout. Train has engine, 3 cars; abt. 11½ in. long. One straight track (6 in.), 8 curved tracks, 2 lead-ons, switch and 6 assorted blocks.

48 T 604—Ship. wt. 2 lbs............Set $3.94

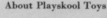

(1) BRIDGE OR OVERPASS. Abt. 14½ in. long.
48 T 585—Ship. wt. 1 lb...............$2.49

(2) TUNNEL. Abt. 5⅞ in. long.
48 T 577—Ship. wt. 10 oz.................98c

(3) TRESTLE BRIDGE. Abt. 9 in. long.
48 T 584—Ship. wt. 8 oz................$1.19

(4) RAILWAY STATION. Abt. 9 in. long.
48 T 587—Ship. wt. 10 oz.................98c

About Playskool Toys

The popular toys on these and the following two pages are scientifically designed so that children *learn while they play.* Beautifully made of wood, constructed for safety, durability. Bright, nontoxic colors. Follow age recommendations, give toys that become fast favorites. Playskool Toys are nationally advertised and sold in finest stores.

Use Your Credit "Charge It" at Wards. See Pg. 279.

Playskool

[A] SPECIAL TOY TRIO—ANY 3 FOR ONLY $4.99. Nationally advertised for $3 to $3.50 each—buy ANY COMBINATION of 3 toys for extra savings.

(1) RURAL MAIL BOX (1½ to 3½ yrs.). The "mailman" drops stenciled blocks that resemble letters and packages in proper slots—then he raises the signal flag and opens the door to collect the mail. Absorbing fun—teaches coordination. All wood, abt. 9¾ in. long. *Nat. adv. at $3.50.*
48 T 574D—Ship. wt. 2 lbs. 8 oz... At Wards $1.88

(2) SPEEDBOAT, TRAILER and SPORTSCAR (2 to 5 yrs.). Exciting wood pull toy for young sportsmen. T-type trailer hitches to car (driver lifts out to "man" the boat). Take-apart cruiser has 3-part hull, detachable "searchlight," "flag," "outboard motor." Abt. 15½ in. long. *Nat. adv. for $3.00.*
48 T 562 D—Ship. wt. 1 lb. 6 oz.... At Wards $1.88

(3) OTTO JACK (1½ to 3½ yrs.). Pump, pump, pump—Jack sticks his head out farther and farther in realistic auto-jack action (will actually lift loads). Pop! suddenly he's back in the box again and the "mechanic" has to repeat the pumping. All wood, abt. 10⅛ in. high. *Nat. adv. at $3.00.*
48 T 607 D—Ship. wt. 1 lb. 12 oz... At Wards $1.88

[B] BAG OF BLOCKS for little builders 2 to 6. Smooth, brightly colored wood—10 assorted shapes, ⅞ in. thick. Mesh bag with drawstring.
48 T 404—Abt. 70 blocks. Ship. wt. 4 lbs. 4 oz.$2.39
48 T 420—About 60 blocks. Natural color finish. Ship. wt. 3 lbs. 8 oz.......................$1.57

[C] FERRY BOAT (1½ to 3½ yrs.). Exciting floor play for the "skipper." Wood boat moves along on hidden wheels, ramps lower for loading and unloading cargo. Two cars and a trailer-truck to roll aboard. Abt. 15⅜ in. long.
48 T 432—Ship. wt. 2 lbs....................$2.39

[D] NOK-OUT BENCH (2 to 5 yrs.). Tots can pound away to their heart's content. Sturdy wood bench has 6 pegs in secret channel—one pops out when mallet hits peg in pounding hole. 6 extra pegs on top. Hardwood top abt. 10 in. long.
48 T 498—Ship. wt. 2 lbs...................$1.75

[E] TAKE-APART TRAIN. *Wards Exclusive.* Fascinating wood "first train" for engineers 3 to 6 to roll along. Engine, coal car, tank car, caboose uncouple. Cars can be taken apart, reassembled (even tiny engineer and fireman lift out). Pull cord.
48 T 588—Abt. 28 in. long. Wt. 2 lbs. 12 oz...$2.79

[F] to [H] GOLDEN BOOK PUZZLES AND BLOC... pealing pictures from children's f... books, reproduced from the famous artists' or...

(F) SET OF EIGHT PUZZLES. Children 2 to 8 lo... ting them together. Beginner starts with si... progresses to most difficult. 2 each with 12, 14... pieces. Colorful inlay pressed board plaques.... Girl Saying Grace, Boats, Elephant, Farm Sce... shown: Dog with Puppies, The Three Bear... coons, Bronco Buster. Each abt. 8x10 in.
48 T 634—Set of 8. Ship. wt. 3 lbs...........

(G) NESTED BLOCKS (1 to 6 yrs.) Fascinating ... tots, teach ABC's. Well made blocks are o... redwood; lithographed animal alphabet pictu... varnished for long wear. Blocks nest AND ... Largest block abt. 6½ in. square.
48 T 482—Set of 8 Blocks. Ship. wt. 3 lbs. ....

(H) CHANGEABLE PICTURE BLOCKS (2 to 10 yrs... attractive—and with lots of play possibili... blocks have different designs and backgroun... on each side; child can build funny anima... "pictures." Lithographed wood blocks ar... nished for long wear. Each abt. 2⅜x2⅜x1½ ...
48 T 586—Set of 12 Blocks. Ship. wt. 2 lbs....

[J] TOTS' TRAIN AND TRACK SETS (2 to 9 yrs.)... of railroading fun! Sturdy plastic track s... snap together for a variety of layouts. Colorfu... train; 3-in. cars couple, uncouple. Layout Boo...

Advanced Set. Two 4-car Trains. 22 track s... (18-ft. railway). 3 bridges with wood blocks... tensions; yoke, switch, bumper, tunnel, statio...
48 T 672—Ship. wt. 4 lbs. 6 oz...............

Regular Set. One 4-car Train. 14 track sectio... feet). 2 bridges, yoke, bumper, switch, ramp...
48 T 671—Ship. wt. 2 lbs. 4 oz..............

Beginners' Set. One 3-car Train. 9 track sectio... (abt. 7½ ft.), bridge, switch, lead-in ramp.
48 T 666—Shipping wt.
1 lb. 4 oz.........$2.24

But back to the wooden train set. The design was first introduced by Skaneateles [*skan-ee-at-e-les*] Handicrafters, a New York–based company known for its simple, well-crafted products. Like many educational toys of its era, it was marketed primarily to adults rather than children. Its potential lay not in the wide-eyed, delighted reaction it would produce when a child received it, nor in the fulfillment of a promise made through a hyper-charged television commercial. According to the instruction sheet packaged with the set, it "Stimulates . . . Satisfies . . . Teaches . . . Develops . . . Promotes . . . Produces a busy, happy child." Yet like a hand-wringing parent peeking around the corner to make sure her child is taking full advantage of the train's unbounded potential, the writer of the instruction sheet also includes a detailed list of "Play Instructions," such as "push train of cars on and off track or over floor" and "prop up track with blocks for a bridge." Sometimes, it seems, things just can't be left to the imagination.

There are two very different kinds of toy trains

One is made of metal painted to look real . . . The other is made of plain, flat wooden blocks that link together easily. All the young child can do with the realistic train is push one car along the floor. It's too hard to put the cars on the track or hitch them together . . . The wooden block cars are different. He can link a string of them together and admire his long train. Two make a trailer truck. He can pile small blocks on top, call it a freight train and make deliveries. When he is bored with dry land, the blocks become separate boats or a string of barges with a tug. He can go on like this forever.

BENJAMIN SPOCK, *Baby and Child Care*, 1968

All-Star Electric Football Game
Gotham Pressed Steel Corporation
1956

Electric Football

The thrill of victory and the agony of defeat. The tabletop game of Electric Football could be both exhilarating and exasperating. For a boy who wanted to play out his fantasies of gridiron glory as a coach, the player figures of Electric Football were like diminutive Roman gladiators poised to do his bidding in the arena of competition. Setting up your team's formation on the metal tabletop was akin to preparing soldiers for battle. With a flip of a switch, an electronic motor set the table vibrating, bringing the players to life like Frankenstein's monster. As the figures buzzed across the "field," however, their paths often took wildly impulsive turns, producing scrum-like heaps of plastic men. Yet it was this capricious ballet of miniature running backs and linemen—and the unpredictable play action that ensued—that captured the spirit of the game of football itself.

Electric Football was introduced by Tudor Metal Products in 1949, just as the sport was growing in popularity thanks to televised games. Using a vibrating metal table to animate game pieces had been a Tudor staple for car racing games since the 1930s. But when Norman Sas took over the business in 1948, he saw the potential to use the technology for football, and the gamble worked. Although early versions included figures that looked more like simian cyborgs than football players, the game was an immediate success. The aesthetics improved with the help of industrial designer Lee

"An incredibly powerful experience

A big part of Electric Football was what you "brought" to the game. What did you want to get out of it. If you weren't patient enough to set up your team after each play, or try to make your bases work better than they did out of the box, then Electric Football was a drag. And that wasn't an unrealistic way for a nine-year-old to feel. But for some of us, when we lined our players up on the field . . . we wanted that play—fans and all—to happen before our eyes. And that wasn't an unrealistic way for a nine-year-old to feel either. We created our own ways and methods to make that play "happen." When you mix creativity and imagination, then sprinkle in the tactile sensation of handling the players and putting them in just the right place, and finally collect the reward of watching a miniature 3-D NFL world come to life—it was an incredibly powerful experience.

EARL SHORES and RODDY GARCIA, *The Unforgettable Buzz: The History of Electronic Football and Tudor Games*

"I was lucky enough to own one of these games just after they started putting NFL team colors on the game figures. Having had a football since I was five and joining Pop Warner when I was nine, I guess my parents felt an Electric Football game was needed. The strategy seemed obvious if you knew anything about football, but once you started playing this game, it became apparent that strategy was limited at best. You'd set up a beautiful formation, and then the darn players would go, well, wherever they darn well wanted to go. Rules were the same usual football rules but it was evident you had to make some of your own dictates or chaos might ensue. I remember setting the rule that once a player with the ball turned and went the wrong way, the play was over. You had to have some rules like that or someone might end up kicking the game across the house. It was fun because it was electronic and it was football.

DARYLE W. HIER, b. 1959, writer and business owner

Payne, who worked with Tudor to develop more realistic figures with improved directional capacity and a cardboard "stadium" that surrounded the field. In 1967 the National Football League granted Tudor the license for Electric Football, which provided significant income for both the toy maker and the NFL for more than a decade. By the early 1970s, Tudor and its competitors were manufacturing increasingly sophisticated games with more life-like figures and detailed stadium environments with operating scoreboards. But by the late 1970s, the craze for tabletop Electric Football began to subside as kids were lured away by computerized versions of the game.

"

Everything was great . . . until you hit the ON switch and the players scrambled around senselessly—just like real football.
JIM OCKULY, b. 1960,
web content manager

F 4.63

Alpha-1 Ballistic Missile
AMSCO Industries, Inc.
1963

Alpha-1 Ballistic Missile

It doesn't take a rocket scientist to design a toy. Or does it? Introduced in 1958, the Alpha-1 Ballistic Missile was developed by Texaco Experiment, Inc., of Richmond, Virginia, a company that specialized in low-altitude research rockets. The Alpha-1 was inspired by the company's pressurized carbon dioxide Cricket model, which was used by meteorologists to determine low-altitude wind patterns. The toy was the brainchild of Dr. Jerry Burke, a scientist at Texaco Experiment who had helped pioneer the performance-enhancing afterburner used in jet fighters. Burke was convinced that he and his team could create a fuel system for amateur rocketry that wouldn't explode or ignite. Unlike previous toy rockets, which relied upon highly flammable liquids for propulsion, the Alpha-1 used pressurized carbon dioxide gas, made by combining sodium bicarbonate "fuel" and citric acid "oxidizer" with water. The chemicals were safe and could even be consumed.

The Alpha-1 kit sold for about five dollars, including the rocket, launching pad, motor chamber, release latch with lanyard, citric acid and bicarbonate, and glass bottles for mixing the fuel. The fuel and oxidizer were loaded into the nose of the inverted rocket, which was then placed upright on the launcher to begin the reaction. After thirty to forty seconds, the budding rocket scientist stepped back about six feet and pulled a lanyard that unlocked the retainer pawl and allowed the rocket to blast off the pad, transforming the backyard or local park into a launching site.

The Alpha-1 boasted a trajectory of one to two hundred feet, which could make the ten-inch plastic projectile extremely dangerous as it plummeted back to earth like a lawn dart. The missile was not a featherweight, either. It had a rubber nose point, carefully chosen according to Dr. Burke's specifications, which

69

came in handy when the missile landed nose first on paved surfaces. On such occasions the rocket could rebound back up in the air fully twenty feet or more, much to the dismay—or delight—of the rocketeer. When making an inverted landing on grass, it was not uncommon for the missile to become embedded up to its fins. Designers of the Alpha-1 were trying for safety, though. In addition to using a nontoxic fuel source, they incorporated protective features in the ignition mechanism to prevent rupture of the missile body, realizing that kids would inevitably push the boundaries by loading in more chemicals to boost the altitude.

ALPHA-1 BALLISTIC MISSILE
AND REMOTE LAUNCHER

The perfect Christmas gift for older boys

The ALPHA-1 actually soars over 150 feet by true rocket propulsion! It's designed by missile engineers and is ready for the count down! The ALPHA-1 is a quality missile made by Scientific Products Company and is powered by completely safe propellants.

$4.98

Everything necessary for many exciting launchings

THE ALPHA-1 BALLISTIC MISSILE SET INCLUDES:

- 10" ALPHA-1 Missile with Rubber Nose Cone
- Remote Launcher
- Non Toxic-Non Flammable "Fuel" and "Oxidizer"
- Storage Tank
- Dilution Tank
- Remote Release Cord
- Launcher Pivot Pin
- Carrying Case
- Launching Manual

Additional "Fuel" Kits, 35c

AVAILABLE AT ANY GOOD TOY OR DEPARTMENT STORE

The Missile Age

The introduction of the Alpha-1 was timely in 1958. The popularity of amateur rocketry had grown considerably during the late 1950s as the space race between the United States and the Soviet Union began to heat up. The successful launch of the Soviet satellite *Sputnik* in 1957 convinced many Americans that the United States had lost the lead in education and technology to the Russians. "The schools are in terrible shape, what has long been an ignored national problem, *Sputnik* has made a recognized crisis," wrote novelist Sloan Wilson in a 1958 *Life* magazine essay on the state of American education. The "educator-approved" Alpha-1 was but one of many toys introduced in the post-*Sputnik* 1950s to get American kids hooked on science.

So, how did I get interested in science and make it my life's work? The first part was fate. The day after the [1957] Ruskin Heights [Missouri] tornado my mom drove me through the damage and I was fascinated by what nature brought. But, that interest was sustained because kids in the late '50s and '60s could get toys that complemented that interest. For example, my friends and I loved my Alpha-1 Ballistic Missile: Mix up some baking soda and vinegar, put it into the missile, put it on the launch pad, and pull the string. That baby could really fly!

MIKE SMITH, b. 1952, meteorologist

Poor, Pitiful Pearl
Brookglad Corporation
1957–60

Poor, Pitiful Pearl

Part of the fun of owning a doll is in the care and tending—the endless changes of clothes, the hair styling, the improvised makeup and nail polish. But for the typical doll, such activities are optional.

Not so with Poor, Pitiful Pearl, a delightfully unkempt little thing measuring a foot tall and meant to pull at the heartstrings of young caretakers. Though Pearl was made by multiple companies and clad in multiple ensembles, she was always sold with a patched dress, dark socks and shoes, and a kerchief. Made of soft vinyl, she could sit, stand, bend, and kneel as she was transformed from grubby to glamorous. "Make her pretty!" read the instructions on the Horsman version of Pearl, introduced in the early 1960s. "Make her wish come true!"

Pearl was sold with a storybook by William Steig, a cartoonist who produced thousands of drawings and more than a hundred covers for the *New Yorker* magazine beginning in 1930. Later in life, Steig began writing and illustrating children's books. He won a Caldecott Medal for *Sylvester and the Magic Pebble* in 1969, and his 1990 picture book *Shrek!* was the basis for a popular animated film. *Poor, Pitiful Pearl* was his early foray into the world of children. The brief story begins with Pearl standing near a bucket, mop in hand, her face and clothing covered with dirt. "What she needs—" the book reads, "is a refreshing bath, a hair-do, a nice dress, clean socks, new shoes, a chance to admire herself." The final illustration depicts Pearl posing in her party dress, hair pinned back, a satisfied smile on her face.

The book ends with two pages of suggested hairdos for Pearl. On one level, it's certainly a lesson in the benefits of good grooming. But the real beauty of this doll is that she doesn't have

A true friend to a little tomboy with scabby knees

It wasn't that I was particularly pitiful, but there was no way I could identify with glamour dolls (like the swish Revlon doll). Pearl helped me accept that most of us were made up of both our black-shoe and bandana times as well as the possibility of shining with a bit of dash. She was a plain doll with a wry, knowing smile, and a true friend to a little tomboy with scabby knees and a wish NOT to have to wear high heels.

ANNIE STANFIELD-HAGERT, b. 1949, clinical social worker

to stay well groomed forever. Once she's done wearing her party frock, Pearl can go back to her comfortable, everyday clothes, and maybe even get them mussed up. Her contemporaries Barbie, Midge, and the gang, doomed to a lifetime of high fashion and higher heels, must have been envious.

Several companies made versions of Poor, Pitiful Pearl. Horsman Dolls— known for popular character dolls including Mary Poppins and Patty Duke— introduced its version in the early 1960s.

The 1960s

Robert J. Smith III

ABC brought the suburban nuclear family into the space age when it premiered *The Jetsons* in 1962. Set one hundred years in the future, the cartoon quenched *Sputnik*-era viewers' thirst for the high-tech wares of 2062 and inspired them to visualize a future of time-saving gadgets, instantaneous transportation, and robotic housekeepers. Yet, despite its technological futurism, *The Jetsons* didn't stray far from traditional norms.

In the opening sequence, we find the family on their morning commute via flying car driven by patriarch George Jetson. One by one, he drops off his boy Elroy at elementary school, daughter Judy at senior high, and Jane, his wife, at the shopping mall. In a hackneyed comedic flourish, Jane traipses off with the hard-earned money George makes as a middle manager at Spacely Space Sprockets. Add in a firecracker boss and a loving dog, and you have all the fixings for a true-blue American family sitcom. In each thirty-minute episode, the good life goes galactic with technology taking care of even the most quotidian human activities. Surely some of the high-tech devices in the Jetson home are meant to be laughed at and not actually cov-

1960

Four black students from North Carolina Agricultural and Technical University in Greensboro stage a sit-in to protest segregation at a Woolworth's lunch counter. Five months later, the counter serves its first black customer.

1961

In his televised farewell address, President Dwight D. Eisenhower warns of the growing power of the "military-industrial complex."

eted, but, nonetheless, *The Jetsons* imagined a utopian world of abundance and easy living made possible by the constant advance of technology and prosperity.

Back on Earth, Americans in the 1960s were wrestling with the harsher reality that, despite the new conveniences of modern life and the real benefits of technological change, indeed we lived in a world of scarce resources, ossified institutions, and differences that were difficult to reconcile. Historians and commentators have called the 1960s many things: an age of great dreams, years of hope, a civil war, revolutionary, a rebellion, and an unraveling—as if the nation were a beloved garment wearing at the seams. Indeed, for the decade's radicals, the nation was in need of repair, of being taken apart and mended into new shapes. The conservative ascendency of Barry Goldwater and Ronald Reagan and the evangelicalism of Billy Graham grew alongside the more well-known ferment on the Left. The institutions of the Right, of the "Silent Majority," speak loud and clear into the present. Alas, it was not the feminist or the Black Panther or the long-haired youth but the Middle American who was named *Time*'s Man and Woman of the Year in 1969: "The mysteries of space were nothing, after all, compared with the menacing confusions of their own society."

While the United States' technological prowess fueled its economic and military rise throughout the Cold War era, the

1962

Helen Gurley Brown, who would later become editor of *Cosmopolitan* magazine, publishes the best-selling advice book *Sex and the Single Girl*.

1963

Hundreds of thousands gather on the National Mall for the signal event of the civil rights movement, the March on Washington for Jobs and Freedom.

1964

In his first State of the Union address, President Lyndon B. Johnson declares his "War on Poverty."

human impact of a future intimately shaped by technology began to emerge in the '60s. Rachel Carson's groundbreaking *Silent Spring* launched investigations into man-made ecological problems, breathing new life into the environmental movement. Innovative organ transplants saved lives and extended them. The napalm dropped by the U.S. military gave us some of the most gruesome images from the American War in Vietnam. The Pill awakened new sexual mores and offered women the power to control their own reproduction. And then, in 1969, the United States put a man on the moon. Scientific advances offered us ways to improve lives and ease human suffering but also gave us new tools to wreak havoc on people and our planet.

Some resisted the allure of technological "progress" by valorizing the benefits of opting out. Perhaps best known for turning their backs on modern life were those who adopted hippie lifestyles. Others, like advocates of the back-to-the-land movement, traded urban and suburban life, with its dependence on electronic conveniences, commuting, and food from distant sources, for a hands-on approach to self-sufficient living. The artists of the 1960s engaged with notions of science and technology, only to turn them on their head—in the unapologetic fashion that characterized the time. The dark comedy *Dr. Strangelove or: How I Learned to Stop Worrying and Love the Bomb*—directed by Stanley Kubrick, the famed filmmaker of *2001: A Space Odys-*

1965

The British Invasion marches on as the Beatles perform the first stadium rock concert in history at New York City's Shea Stadium.

1966

Entertainment titan Walt Disney dies at the age of sixty-five.

sey, *The Shining*, *A Clockwork Orange*, and other classics—tried to laugh us into awareness with its satirical take on Cold War nuclear brinkmanship.

And in a matter-of-fact manner all his own, Black Power poet Gil Scott-Heron challenged us through frank juxtaposition: "I can't pay no doctor bill, but Whitey's on the moon."

For Further Reading

Rachel Carson, *Silent Spring*

Matthew D. Lassiter, *The Silent Majority: Suburban Politics in the Sunbelt South*

Lisa McGirr, *Suburban Warriors: The Origins of the New American Right*

Gil Scott-Heron, *Now and Then: The Poems of Gil Scott-Heron*

Matthew Wisnioski, *Engineers for Change: Competing Visions of Technology in 1960s America*

1967

The Green Bay Packers defeat the Kansas City Chiefs in the first AFL-NFL World Championship Game, now known as Super Bowl I.

1968

A large group of feminist women gather in Atlantic City, New Jersey, to protest the Miss America beauty pageant, garnering significant media attention for the women's liberation movement.

1969

The Docuteller, the nation's first automatic teller machine (ATM), is installed at the Chemical Bank in Rockville Centre, New York.

Giant Troll Bank
Dam Trolls
1964

Trolls

Fads seem to come out of nowhere. You're contentedly skipping rope in your driveway, and then a kid shows up with a Hula-Hoop and you're hopelessly passé. You love your felt cowboy hat and spurs until, all of a sudden, everyone else has an authentic Davy Crockett coonskin cap and you just have to have one, too. You're playing with Barbie and Ken, and then your friend shows up with an ugly-cute little alternative, and you wonder how you can possibly go on without one.

Like the mischievous characters of Scandinavian folklore that inspired them, the origin of troll dolls is the stuff of legend. In 1952 Helena and Martti Kuuskoski introduced a line of dolls called FAUNI-trolls in their native Finland. Each of their handmade dolls had its own personality, story, and appearance. While FAUNI-trolls continue to have a strong following, it was Thomas Dam, a Danish baker who enjoyed woodcarving in his spare time, whose creations seem to have sparked the 1960s fad. In 1956 Dam began selling comical carved animals and caricatures of old men and women door to door. His efforts paid off when a Swedish department store hired him to create their Christmas window displays. Dam sculpted a row of trolls out of rubber, then inserted a spring in each one. He attached the dolls to a plank of wood that moved, so that his trolls appeared to be waving and jumping up and down on their perch. Created simply to lure customers into the store, the trolls sparked something of a buying frenzy. Customers couldn't wait to get their hands on the creatures.

Fast forward a year, and Dam, his wife, and his daughter are working around the clock to meet demand for their rubber trolls (now without springs inside), each one a little marvel with an endearing grin and dyed wool hair. In 1959 they broke ground on a factory in their hometown of Gjol, Denmark, and formed Dam

Things Entertainment. Over the next few years they moved from rubber to molded plastic (PVC, to be exact), opened additional factories in New Zealand and Florida, and watched their glassy-eyed creatures take over the world.

In 1964 Dam issued a license to make trolls to Uneeda Doll Company, a Brooklyn-based firm in business since 1917. Uneeda launched its "Wishnik" line of trolls that year, promising that all who stroked the dolls' hair would enjoy a run of good luck. Lots of other companies jumped on the bandwagon, too, and at the height of the craze there were troll pencil toppers, key chains, lunch boxes, and more. Trolls popped up in dorm rooms, they hung from rearview mirrors, and they were even given as wedding gifts. The fad disappeared as quickly as it began—but thank goodness there are still plenty of 1960s trolls around today, reminders of a decade when some crazy hair and a big grin could really get you places.

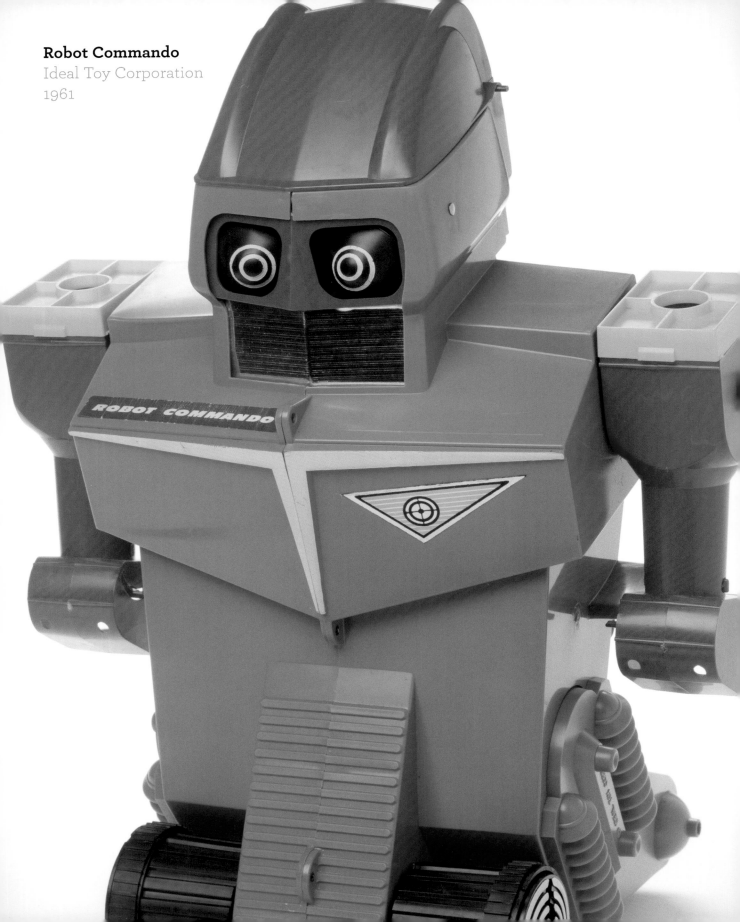

Robot Commando
Ideal Toy Corporation
1961

Robot Commando

By the time Robot Commando premiered in 1961, toy robots had a strong foothold on America's toy shelves. In an attempt to rebuild Japan's economy after World War II, many products—including toys—that had once been made in the United States were sent to Japan for manufacturing. Importers then purchased Japanese toys for sale to American customers. By the mid-1950s, Japan had become a leading manufacturer of toys, including a steady stream of brightly colored tin robots with detailed features that hinted of their origins in outer space.

The popularity of these Japanese imports was fueled by a nationwide mania for science fiction comics and films. From the stories of Isaac Asimov, Arthur C. Clarke, and Robert Heinlein to blockbuster movies like *Forbidden Planet* (featuring the uber-competent Robby the Robot), chronicles of life beyond Earth were an established part of the midcentury American cultural landscape.

Robot Commando arrived at the tail end of this wave, as American attention was shifting from a fictional view of life beyond planet Earth to the very real prospect of sending humans into space. The launching of the Soviet *Sputnik* satellite in 1957 inspired a flurry of space-related toys; NASA-themed toys grew in popularity throughout the 1960s. With his sturdy, nineteen-inch-tall plastic frame, Robot Commando stood poised on the cusp of a new era. Like his predecessors—including Ideal's 1954 hit Robert the Robot—Robot Commando walked, turned right or left, and emitted strangely satisfying noises, all commands dispatched via a remote controller tethered to his back. But there was more. As his name implied, Robot Commando was a fighter, equipped with plastic balls that shot from his swinging arms and small rockets that fired from his head. "He's your one-man Army," children were assured through a television commercial

Isaac Asimov introduced his Three Rules of Robotics in the 1942 short story "Runaround." The rules were meant as a unifying theme for Asimov's robot-related fiction, but they're also useful in the world of robot play:

1. A robot may not injure a human being or, through inaction, allow a human being to come to harm.

2. A robot must obey the orders given to it by human beings, except where such orders would conflict with the First Law.

3. A robot must protect its own existence as long as such protection does not conflict with the First or Second Law.

depicting Robot Commando marching through a deserted city, fending off attacks from tanks and airplanes. "He takes orders from no one but you."

Soon enough, children of the 1960s were confronted with images of real danger, signs of an instability upsetting to their elders. A president speaking of the threat of nuclear war. That same president shot and killed in the clear light of day. Images of war appearing each night on the evening news. Robot Commando was a primary-colored protector in an increasingly confusing world.

**Rotate-O-Matic
Super Astronaut**
Horikawa
1960s

If you wanted to point to one thing in my life that sparked a lasting interest in mechanics and engineering, this is it

When you opened that plastic skull, you had direct access to all the gears, cams, pulleys, rods, and wires within. I must have ripped off half the skin on my hands trying to reach in and examine how all that apparatus worked. I eventually broke it . . . My mother was mad but my father and I took it as an opportunity for applied screwdrivers and hex wrenches. Marvelous time with old Dad, but the surgery was not successful. From then on, I supplied the motion and the noise to the toy myself.

JIM ECKBERG, b. 1957, marketing communications consultant

Barbie and Ken
Mattel, Inc.
1962

Barbie

From the Love Generation to Generation Y, she's seen it all. She's done it all, too, with a résumé that includes fashion model, firefighter, engineer, surgeon, astronaut, rock star, summit diplomat, and presidential candidate. She's the ultimate cultural chameleon, transforming herself from a miniskirted '60s Mod to a denim-clad '70s hippie chick. Her signature golden locks have sported every conceivable hairstyle from bubble cut to pageboy. She's one of the most intoxicating pop culture icons of the twentieth century, the subject of scores of books, articles, and even college courses. She's the Babe Ruth of post–World War II toys. And her name is Barbie.

When Mattel cofounder Ruth Handler suggested an adult-bodied female doll to company executives in the early 1950s, they were less than enthusiastic. After all, infant dolls had dominated the market for decades and fit the bill in preparing young girls for their future roles as mothers. But when Handler noticed her daughter Barbara (Barbie's namesake) giving adult roles to paper dolls during play, she knew there was a niche to be filled. Handler was in Europe in 1956 when she spotted a blonde-haired, long-legged doll named Bild Lilli, after a German cartoon strip character. Lilli was a sassy, independent working girl, and her womanly figure was just what Handler envisioned for her doll. Mattel took cues from the Lilli doll and adapted its own design, which appeared as Barbie in 1959. Marketed as a "Teen-age fashion model," Barbie was the first mass-produced toy in America with adult features and was an instant success, with 350,000 dolls sold in the first year of production. Mattel was a pioneer in television advertising, being the first toy maker to broadcast commercials directly to kids in 1955 as a sponsor for the *Mickey Mouse Club* program. Soon after her debut, Barbie commercials began to saturate children's primetime TV programming, and sales skyrocketed.

> **In the early '70s,** *I received my first Barbie doll when I was eight years old. Then came Ken and several others until I had quite a collection. These dolls were not only toys to me, but an extended family. I spent many, many hours with them every day for years. They had a permanent home against my bedroom wall that stretched six feet long. Everyone had a bed complete with linens and pillows that my mother had made. I used the Sears catalogs as the foundations. The kitchen was furnished with all sorts of dishes, pots, pans, and an array of "food." The living room had a TV I made from an old cardboard jewelry box that I drew on and a newspaper I cut out from an old magazine. I had the Corvette, RV, and swimming pool, also. Every holiday was celebrated with them, down to a pine-tree branch decorated with popcorn at Christmastime.*
> CONNIE QUINN, b. 1965

"A world where everything good was possible for Barbie and me"

As a child, there were only two toys that I wanted above all others—an Easy-Bake Oven and a Barbie doll. Since my parents continually rejected the oven because of safety issues, they agreed to Barbie. My first Barbie was the original "Twist 'n Turn Waist" model, and she had long blonde hair and an orange bikini with a mesh oversuit. I can still remember how excited I was to receive that doll! Pretty soon, I acquired her sisters, Skipper and Tutti, her cousin, Francie, and her friends Stacie, P.J., Ken, and Casey, several houses, and a car. I saved all of my Christmas and birthday money to buy them clothes and other accessories—and my collection just kept growing. I loved those dolls so much because they provided me a distraction from problems at home, especially my pesky little brother, and created a world where everything good was possible for Barbie and me. Barbie and her clan were doctors, nurses, teachers, singers, actors, writers, homemakers, fashion designers, lawyers, and chefs. They helped me re-enact scenes from a favorite story on my own or served as props for a book report or other project at school. Growing up, I was known as "the girl with the cleanest, neatest Barbies" in my neighborhood. If anyone tried to play with one of my dolls when their hands were dirty, they were promptly directed to the soap and sink to wash up!

JANICE FISHER

I can honestly say that I have been a fan since 1959, the year that Barbie was "born." I was only three, but I had an older sister who waited patiently for Perry Brothers Five & Dime in Lufkin [Texas] to replenish their supply that had sold out in one day. We had both asked Santa for the doll. My sister wanted the blonde doll, and she told me that I wanted the brunette. When we finally brought our Barbies home, we were so excited. We realized that we had to have more money so that we could buy clothes. So we went to our aunt's house and asked for her old drink bottles that could be returned for the deposit, and we walked across the street with bottles in hand and left the store with $2.05 in cash. That bought us a dress each, and we were very happy little girls. Our collection grew with every chore, returnable bottle deposit, birthday, or Christmas. I remember my mother sitting on our front porch sewing Barbie-sized buttons on the new outfit that she was finishing. I remember looking down the street, waiting patiently for my friends Datha and Tonya to start walking from their houses with Barbie case in hand. Countless days we sat on the porch, combining our Barbie clothes so that we would have a greater mix, making Barbie furniture out of old match boxes, shoe boxes, or whatever we could find. It was such a wonderful, simple time.

KATHY BUNKLEY, b. 1956, secretary

By 1961 consumer demand had reached such a fever pitch that Mattel released a new doll. Barbie's boyfriend Ken (named after Handler's son) appeared in March of that year, clad in red swim trunks and sporting "molded" plastic hair. Like Barbie, Ken has transformed his appearance over the years, particularly in the grooming department, which reached its pinnacle in 1973 with a rooted hairstyle for Mod Hair Ken. Barbie's coterie continued to grow with the introduction of best friend Midge in 1963 and little sister Skipper in 1964.

More than 800 million Barbies have been sold worldwide, but being the most popular doll in history hasn't always been easy. With a seemingly endless stash of clothing, cars, and "Dream Houses," Barbie has been branded as a poster child for materialism, and many claim that her supermodel-on-steroids good looks and unrealistic body proportions have created unachievable expectations for young girls. Others defend Barbie as a positive influence who provided an alternative to the traditional gender roles of the 1950s, a point echoed by her creator. "My whole philosophy of Barbie," said Ruth Handler, "was that through the doll, the little girl could be anything she wanted to be. Barbie always represented the fact that a woman has choices." Whatever her fate, there's no denying that Barbie has played a significant role as both a mirror and a model of American culture.

Mouse Trap
Ideal Toy Corporation
1963

Mouse Trap

Is it a board game or a machine? Do you follow the game rules or just assemble the elaborate contraption for the sheer fun of setting it in motion?

Mouse Trap was an instant hit after its 1963 debut. By year's end, Ideal had sold more than 1.2 million of the games. As one of the first three-dimensional board games to hit the market, Mouse Trap lured potential players with the promise of a quirky quest: "It's fun to build this comical wonder," read the game's catchphrase, "but woe to the mouse who gets caught under." The game includes twenty-two plastic parts, ranging from a bathtub to a rickety staircase, a rubber band, a steel marble, a plastic ball, and a spring. As players move their plastic mice around the board, they are prompted to combine the parts into an elaborate mousetrap. Once the trap is completed, a lucky player sets it in motion, trapping the unfortunate mice of his opponents.

The game was the brainchild of Marvin Glass, a giant of twentieth-century toy design whose Marvin Glass and Associates trademark appeared on an astounding number of hits, including Mr. Machine, Operation, Rock 'Em Sock 'Em Robots, and Lite Brite. Less an inventor than an instigator, Glass led a talented staff of designers and engineers who transformed his ideas into workable, marketable products.

Glass's inspiration for Mouse Trap came from the drawings of Rube Goldberg, a Pulitzer Prize–winning cartoonist. An engineer who began his career with San Francisco's water and sewers department, Goldberg poured his talents into a popular syndicated newspaper cartoon series. He was best known for his tongue-in-cheek blueprints for such necessaries as "Self-Shining Shoes." Look up "Rube Goldberg" in the dictionary, and you'll see that he's become an adjective for "a contrivance that brings about by complicated means what apparently could have been accomplished simply."

Goldberg's designs were never meant to be built. And Glass's genius was in recognizing that a game can be about more than winning. There's no mad fortune to be made through Mouse Trap, no mystery to be solved, no score card to keep. The delight is in taking the time to build a haphazard machine that, once set in motion, may or may not achieve its desired result. Will the steel ball really fall into the bathtub? Will the old man really jump into the washtub? For the millions who have played Mouse Trap over the years, the real question is, "When can we try it again?"

How to Get Rid of a Mouse

The best mousetrap by Rube Goldberg: Mouse (A) dives for painting of cheese (B), goes through canvas and lands on hot stove (C). He jumps on cake of ice (D) to cool off. Moving escalator (E) drops him on boxing glove (F) which knocks him into basket (G) setting off miniature rocket (H) which takes him to the moon.

THiS SeCTiON CONTAiNS

GeaR 3
DiViNG BoaRD
GeaR SUPPORT
PLUMBiNG
MoUSe TRaP
Base C
THiNG-a-Ma-JiG
BaTHTUB
STOP SiGN
RaiN GUTTeR

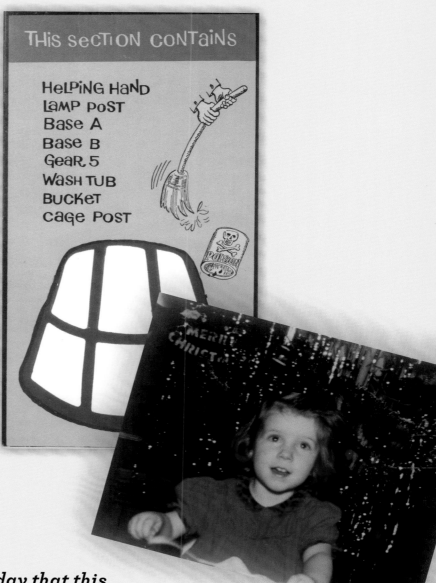

THiS SeCTiON CONTAiNS

HeLPiNG HaND
LaMP PoST
Base A
Base B
GeaR 5
WaSH TUB
BUCKeT
CaGe PoST

POISON

> ## "
> ### *Oh, how I dreamed of the day that this would be in our house!*
>
> *This along with Operation and the John and Jane West dolls (with their horses and all their tack) were part of a suite of toys that never, ever made it into my house. Too many parts to lose, too expensive, and frankly too cool for my parents to even think of buying. We got puzzles, Sorry, and the game that came the closest, Clue. But oh, how I dreamed of the day that this would be in our house. If they had only gotten it for me, I would have become an engineer, I'm sure of it.*
>
> TERRY SCHELLER, b. 1959, full-time graphic specialist, part-time goofball

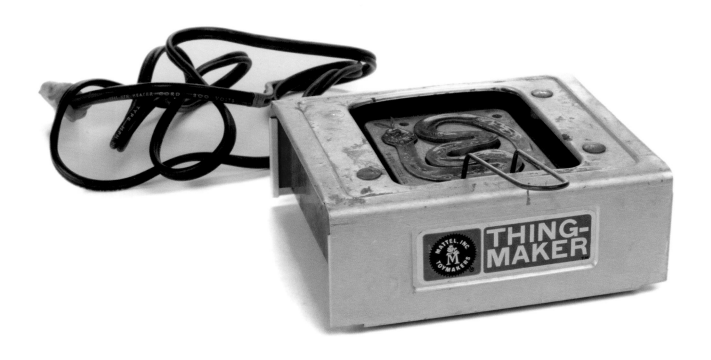

Thingmaker

Mattel, Inc.

1964–66

Thingmaker

A toy that creates more toys. Could it be every kid's dream? Edgar Burns, an engineer working for Mattel in the early 1960s, certainly thought it was. Burns joined Mattel in 1963, when the company was riding high on the success of the Barbie doll and needed a toy that would appeal to boys. In 1962 Mattel had introduced a plastic molding machine called the Vac-U-Form, in which heated plastic was vacuum-molded over a form to create everything from boats and cars to log cabins. Burns took the process a step further by developing metal molds and liquid plastic compounds that could be used with a freestanding heater, thus allowing children to make their own toys. The bosses at Mattel liked the idea and christened it the Thingmaker.

Introduced in 1964, the Thingmaker delighted kids who could cast their own rubbery bugs, creatures, and other concoctions by heating and curing a liquefied polyvinyl chloride compound dubbed Plastigoop. Mattel introduced the Maker-Pak series of packaged molds that same year, starting with Creepy Crawlers, which featured a variety of spiders, roaches, caterpillars, and centipedes. Butterflies, dragonflies, and moths—also included in the series—could be fitted with plastic cutout wings using a "wing template."

With the success of Creepy Crawlers, Mattel launched additional Maker-Paks for its Thingmaker, including Fighting Men (miniature plastic soldiers), Creeple People (head, feet, and arms for attaching to pencils), and Fright Factory (shrunken heads, anyone?). In 1966 Mattel set their Thingmaker sights on girls with the Flower Fun Maker-Pak, which made plastic petals and posies, and grid-patterned artwork molds called Picadoos. Incredible Edibles, which featured the same bugs and creatures as Creepy Crawlers, was also introduced in 1966, but with a twist: the Plastigoop was replaced by four flavors of Gobble-Degoop

In November 1967 Mattel briefly removed Incredible Edibles from the market after reports that diabetic children had become ill. The starch in the product converted into sugar when digested. A new sugar-free version with a warning label was quickly introduced in time for Christmas.

(root beer, licorice, cinnamon, and butterscotch), which allowed kids to eat their ghoulish creations. Mattel even created Thingmaker molds to replicate licensed characters like the Peanuts cartoon gang and superheroes including Batman, Superman, and the Green Hornet.

Although popular with kids, the Thingmaker could be a parent's nightmare. Operating a hot plate oven that heated molten plastic to 390 degrees left the house with noxious odors and many children with burned fingers, and by the early 1970s the toy was removed from store shelves. In 1992 the Thingmaker line was resurrected by ToyMax with a safer heating source and a new Plastigoop formula. JAKKS Pacific purchased ToyMax in 2002 and continues to market Creepy Crawlers through its Flying Colors subsidiary.

"Hot metal and toxic fumes— what more could a kid want?"

When I was a kid, a lot of girls I knew had Easy-Bake Ovens. For boys, the opportunity to give yourself second-degree burns and burn your house down came via the Thingmaker. As part of the monster craze of the 1960s—sparked by the TV reissue of the old Universal monster movies, which also precipitated Famous Monsters of Filmland magazine—Mattel released the Thingmaker Fright Factory in 1966. With the Thingmaker, boys could make realistic scars, fangs, eyeballs, miniature skeletons, and, oddest of all, shrunken heads. The scars and eyeballs could be applied—hopefully after they cooled—directly to your skin to excite and alarm your parents. The skeleton could be assembled. The shrunken heads . . . well, I'm not sure what you could do with them other than freak out squeamish girls who had been waiting several hours for a light bulb to bake a cake. I loved my Thingmaker but remain to this day surprised that it was allowed to come to the market. My mom, a smart woman, wouldn't let me use it in the house. No doubt remembering the Silly Putty Incident of 1967—which left a stiff, permanent stain on our carpet—she banished me and my Thingmaker to our front porch.

KEITH ROYSDON, b. 1959, journalist

My Fun Flower Kit was the cat's meow: a large box filled with cast aluminum molds, assorted colors of Plastigoop, the infamous Thingmaker, and enough possibilities to keep me busy for hours. For a nine-year-old, it was magic. With the exception of a few burns now and then, I had full ownership of the process from start to finish: gently squeezing Plastigoop into the proper mold, carefully monitoring the transformation of goop into flowers and butterflies, transferring the hot metal cast to a cooling tray, followed by the satisfaction of prying the finished product from the mold. Flowers and butterflies for everyone! In hindsight, I see that the Thingmaker fed all of what I value today: creativity, thoughtful planning, and philanthropy.

SHERRI GEBERT FULLER, b. 1957, corporate/foundation gift officer

Easy-Bake Oven
Kenner Products
1963

Easy-Bake Oven

At first blush, the notion of a working oven for young children seems like a crazy idea. It runs contrary to everything we are taught as kids about the "grown-up" stove in the kitchen, which we are supposed to avoid unless we want burnt fingers, hair, clothes, etc. But therein lies the brilliance behind the Easy-Bake Oven. Introduced in 1963, it wasn't the first electric toy oven. Toy train manufacturer Lionel marketed an electric stove in 1930, and the Metal Ware Corporation of Two Rivers, Wisconsin, had manufactured its "Little Lady" toy range since the 1940s. But these products were miniature versions of actual appliances, which were a genuine safety hazard to children. The Easy-Bake, patterned after ovens used by pretzel vendors, had a port into which mix-laden bakeware could be inserted for cooking and cooling, and the heating source consisted of two 100-watt light bulbs tucked safely into the oven—both features a relief to parents.

Marketed with the slogan "Just like Mom's—bake your cake and eat it too!" the Easy-Bake Oven featured a wide variety of premixed (just add water) bake sets for preparing all sorts of confectionery delights, including cakes, cookies, fudge, pretzels, candy bars, and even bubble gum. More than 500,000 ovens were sold in the first year, prompting Kenner to release twenty-five additional bake sets over the next three years, including a TV dinner–style offering in 1965 consisting of beef macaroni with peas and carrots. As the food mixes evolved to accommodate changing palates, so did the aesthetics and functionality of the oven. The 1960s turquoise color gave way to avocado green and harvest gold versions in the 1970s, and in the 1980s the traditional range facade was discontinued and replaced with a profile that kids could relate to: the microwave. Even the oven's heating source—the incandescent light bulb—would eventually be replaced by a dedicated heating element.

"The bakery to beat all bakeries

Some of my most memorable recollections of my childhood include memories with my friends. For instance, I have this really vivid memory of cooking with my Easy-Bake Oven. For me this was the toy of all toys. It came with real baking mix (just add water), pans to cook with, and a plug-in oven that baked via a light bulb! All on a miniature scale, of course, the perfect size for a seven-year-old. I liked it because, as a young girl, I could independently bake muffins, cookies, and cakes without the assistance of my mom. It was a great toy! What I enjoyed even more than the independence of cooking without mom's help, however, was baking with friends. I would have a girl friend or two come over, and together we would create the bakery to beat all bakeries (at least we thought so) and have the neighborhood kids and my brothers sample the goods. I remember playing "make believe" as we baked up a storm. We pretended we were world-renowned bakers baking for the Partridge family and their friends the Bradys. Or we imagined we had a dinner party in an hour and "everyone" was going to be there. In our pretend bakery we baked for a wedding, a birthday, a party, a carnival, even a school lunch. We did it all because we had amazing abilities, we were friends, and we had an Easy-Bake Oven.

KAREN CREASEY, b. 1962, speaker and writer

Aww, I loved mine! You had to send away for the little boxes of mixes. Waiting for them to come from the mailman was an eight-year-old's introduction to the concept of eternity. I would proudly make "dessert" for the family, but usually by serving time, I had very carefully finger-swiped all the pink frosting off the tiny cake. It also made strange little rubber candy blobs. To this day I am not sure they were really food. The toy did sear into my brain the physics behind incandescent light and infrared heat. The new ones have lost the magic light bulbs, as now a hot light bulb and pans from the oven are considered "too dangerous!" No, you also learned about the physics of not touching hot things! (Although this is something you probably learned before you were old enough to mix cake.)

EVA TERRELL, b. 1959, archaeologist

The marketing strategy for the Easy-Bake also changed with the times. In keeping with conventional gender roles of the 1960s, the toy was initially advertised solely to girls, with boys serving primarily as consumers of the baked goods. Forty years later, an Easy-Bake spin-off called the Queasy Bake Cookerator was launched, offering boys the chance to get busy in the kitchen making such detestable delectables as Mud 'n Crud Cakes and Drip and Drool Dog Bones. Despite all these transformations, the Easy-Bake's popularity hasn't waned, and with more than 23 million sold, it continues to endure as a source of inspiration for aspiring young chefs.

Betty Crocker mixes for the Easy-Bake Oven were introduced in 1968 after General Mills purchased Kenner Products.

Rat Fink
Revell Company
1964

Rat Fink

Nineteen-sixty-three was not the best of years for Mickey Mouse. Sure, kids could still tune into Annette, Bobby, and the rest of the Mouseketeers on weekday afternoons—but only in reruns, airing after *American Bandstand,* the show that captivated American teens by presenting kids just like themselves dancing to Top 40 hits and chatting with host Dick Clark. Meanwhile, a new rodent was capturing the attention of America's youth. And man, he sure wasn't from Disneyland.

Rat Fink was a crazed-looking mouse with bloodshot eyes and sharp, gnarly teeth. His creator, Ed "Big Daddy" Roth, is said to have conceived of him as an anti-Mickey. A cartoonist and custom car designer who was a key player in southern California's hot rod scene in the 1950s and '60s, Roth began airbrushing and selling "Weirdo" T-shirts in the late 1950s. Featuring a stable of unsavory creatures riding in souped-up machines, the T-shirts became hugely popular.

Roth's Rat Fink T-shirt was first advertised in the July 1963 issue of *Car Craft* magazine. That same year, Revell introduced a Rat Fink model kit, the first of twelve in their successful if short-lived Roth Monsters line. The company had already made a big splash with their "Outlaw" car, modeled on one of Roth's custom designs. Worried that this left turn into the world of toys— guaranteed to delight kids while offending their parents—might damage Revell's wholesome image, the company appointed a committee to study the effects of monster toys on America's youth. After noting the committee's conclusion—that monsters help youngsters cope with life's problems—Revell introduced kids to other members of the Roth gang, including Drag Nut, Mr. Gasser, and Mother's Worry.

Revell and Roth weren't the only ones producing outlandish, grotesque toys in the early 1960s. Aurora Plastics marketed

Flamboyant, larger-than-life Ed "Big Daddy" Roth was a ready-made spokesperson for Revell's Roth Monster lineup. But by the late 1960s Roth was riding with outlaw motorcycle gangs, and Revell had dropped him and his line of model toys from their catalogs.

a successful line of Universal movie monsters, including Dracula and Frankenstein. Hawk Model made Weird-Ohs, and Marx made Nutty Mads, a series of crazed six-inch figures with maniacal expressions. Remco countered with a line of disgusting bugs called Horrible Hamiltons. And in 1964, Mattel introduced its Thing-maker, with kits that allowed children to pour plastic goop into molds that popped out Creepy Crawlers and Incredible Edibles.

A unifying theme linked all these toys: Adults did not buy them because they were good for kids. They bought them because, for better or worse, they knew their kids wanted them. More and more since the mid-1950s, toy marketers were speaking directly to kids through their television and print advertisements. Kid culture was becoming increasingly defined as separate from the world of adults. Within a few years, these kids would be the teenagers and young adults who stood on one side of the late-'60s generation gap. Mickey and the gang may have had a more wholesome image, but he and Rat Fink both inhabited worlds designed around and for kids. Maybe those two rodents had something in common after all.

We were seeing rebellion in music and design and wanted our toys to reflect outsiders as well

Stephen Yogi Rueff
at right

Big Daddy Roth was the voice of outsiders and nonconformists of the late '50s in California. By the 1960s, Rat Fink images spread across the country and spoke to and for nonconformists, which resonated with me.

The kids I knew who were hard-core Big Daddy Roth followers were the tough kids in our community and definitely not members of the predominant hippie culture of the University of Minnesota area where I grew up in the '60s. That said, I loved the exaggerated visual style of Big Daddy Roth characters with their twisted physical characteristics and sneering and leering personae. During this time we were seeking ways to rebel against the prescribed conformity reinforced by public school dress codes and the three national tele- vision channels. *We were seeing rebellion in music and design and wanted our toys to reflect outsiders as well.*

The whimsy and surrealist images of Big Daddy Roth's style eventually influenced and reverberated through the mainstream toys world; the hard edges of toys softened. Andy Warhol–inspired Pop art was seen in the Batman *TV series, and dark Edward Gorey / Charles Addams aesthetics started to move into broadcast television in* The Addams Family *and* The Munsters. *Rat Fink and his knock-off brethren gave us role models for accepting outsiders into mainstream images of society.*

STEPHEN YOGI RUEFF, b. 1958, business consultant to cultural nonprofits

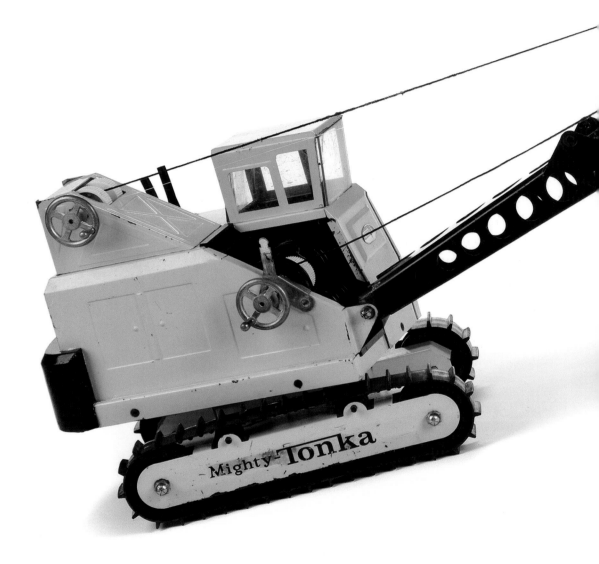

Mighty Tonka Crane and Clam
Tonka Toys, Inc.
1966

Tonka Trucks

In 1946, partners Avery Crounse, Lynn Baker, and Alvin Tesch set out to create a metal implement and tool business on the shores of Lake Minnetonka in Minnesota. They called their company Mound Metalcraft. Fortunately for children everywhere, they were more successful with toys than with gardening tools. Having only a handful of tie racks as merchandise, the men decided their business might need a secondary product and so they tried their hand at metal toys based on designs by Streater Industries, a tooling company that had previously owned the building. The partners made some changes to the former owners' designs and created a logo for the toys using the word *Tonka,* a Dakota Indian word meaning "great" or "large."

The young company produced only two designs in 1947—a crane and a steam shovel—but the toys were a great hit with post–World War II families, and 37,000 units were sold that first year. This huge success led the partners to set aside the garden tool business and make metal toys their primary product.

They focused on manufacturing the most durable toy for the money on the market, and the popularity of Tonka toys skyrocketed. In 1955, as sales continued to climb, the company

I was a true hero

Tonka trucks have inspired and entertained generations of children through the power of play and imagination. And for some kids that first Tonka paved the way for a career and a lifetime fascination for all things truck-like:

Admit it. Your first truck wasn't a Mack; it was a Tonka. Go back to your childhood and remember. Did you find it Christmas morning under the tree with a bright red bow on it? Or, was it a birthday present? Or, did your snotty big brother finally get tired of his and hand it down to you after years of being patient. That's right! You treated and loved that truck better than he ever did! And that Tonka gave you more than just hours of playtime; it gave you your career. Without Tonka, you might have never dreamed of becoming a truck driver, so, alas, we pay homage to the mighty "Tonka Tough."

I had the crane and dump truck and hauled tons of cat litter from construction site to construction site. An extremely important

continued next page

changed its name to Tonka Toys, Inc. The company became part of Hasbro, Inc., in 1991.

While Tonka has produced a variety of toys—everything from dolls to computer games—its most popular model line has been trucks, which were introduced in 1949. A pickup was released in 1955, followed by a jeep in 1962. The Mighty Dump Truck, with its signature vibrant yellow paint job, premiered in 1964 and became the company's best-selling vehicle ever. Its suc-

cess spawned an entire line of Mighty products that continues today. Although the materials have changed (vehicle bodies are now made of hard plastic), Tonka trucks continue to uphold the same premise the brand was founded upon: a toy should be durable and provide children with as much play value as possible.

continued from previous page

haul and, no, the cat litter was not dirty. And, of course, I could not be without the fire trucks. I saved so many lives and put out so many fires with those trucks. I was a true hero, and that's the point of Tonka. Tonka allows young boys'—and girls'— imaginations to run wild. You can be anything you want to be with a Tonka; it doesn't matter as long as you have the right truck, and through the years there have been plenty to choose from. The jingle says it all: "I love dumpin', I love diggin', I love haulin', I love liftin', I love dirt and rocks and sand and mud and muck. I love my Tonka! Man, I love my truck!"

EDWARD GREEN, trucker, author

Frisbee
Wham-O
1966

Frisbee

It all started with a pie plate. Established in 1871, the Frisbie Baking Company of Bridgeport, Connecticut, was renowned for its pies, which were consumed with glee by many college students in the New England area. Students soon discovered that the empty pie tins made excellent flying objects, which could be thrown and caught across campus lawns. The Frisbie, as it became known, was dramatically improved in 1948 by Los Angeles building inspector Walter "Fred" Morrison and his partner, Warren Franscioni, who developed a plastic version that possessed superior throwing accuracy and distance.

In 1955 Fred Morrison launched his own version of the plastic Frisbie, which he named the Pluto Platter in a nod to Americans' growing captivation with science fiction and flying saucers. The outer third of the disk, with its characteristic curve, was later patented by Morrison and became the fundamental design for all Frisbies. Morrison's design captured the attention of Richard Knerr and Arthur "Spud" Melin, owners of the recently formed toy company Wham-O.

In 1957 Wham-O purchased the rights to Morrison's Pluto Platter and began producing more disks under the same name. Eager to increase sales of the new toy, Richard Knerr noodled around for a moniker and came up with the product name Frisbee, a spin-off of the Connecticut bakery that had inadvertently started the craze. Further enhancements to the design, materials, and performance of the disk were made by Wham-O's general manager and vice president of marketing Eddie Headrick, whose patented improvements were dubbed the "Rings of Headrick." When the toy was marketed as a new sport, sales went through the roof, and in 1964 the first "professional" model was introduced. Sales increased again in 1967, when high school students in Maplewood, New Jersey, developed the game of

Ultimate Frisbee, which combines features of football, basketball, and soccer. Frisbee golf, including professional courses and associations, would arrive a decade later, and by 1994—the year Wham-O was sold to Mattel—more than 100 million Frisbees had been purchased.

How it all started: a pie tin from the Frisbie Baking Company (1871–1958)

The Alternative Sport

I can remember my first Frisbee: my father gave it to me right about the time that every American in the country was obsessed with the Hula-Hoop. Back in 1959, my brother and I immediately invented a game that involved a Hula-Hoop, a Frisbee, and a barking cocker spaniel. I think the dog was the referee. My favorite memories of playing with a Frisbee are from college at the University of Houston when I was dating my future wife. My favorite date was the picnic at the park with a Frisbee. I remember a blanket in the park, cold chicken, and tossing a Frisbee until we were so tired we had to go back and lie on the blanket.

MARK MILLIORN, b. 1953, history professor

G.I. Joe Mercury Astronaut
Hasbro, Inc.
1966

G.I. Joe

He's the original action figure toy and has been a bellwether of American culture for nearly half a century. G.I. Joe was conceived by Hasbro in the early 1960s to answer the success its competitor Mattel had achieved with the Barbie doll. Like Barbie, the military-themed dolls could be accessorized with clothing and equipment. Rather than create a different doll for each branch of the military, Hasbro decided to create a generic figure with a masculine and handsome face and a name inspired by the 1945 film *The Story of G.I. Joe* ("Government Issue Joe" was a reference to American servicemen during World War II).

When the figure premiered in 1964, no one had seen anything quite like it. Standing nearly a foot tall, G.I. Joe sported an athletic physique and twenty-one moveable parts, thanks to the inspiration of Don Levine, Hasbro's vice president and director of marketing and development. Levine took the idea from a wooden artist's mannequin he spied in a display window and realized the same concept could be used to create figures that replicate the movements of the human body. Levine was also adamant that this was not to be called a doll—a term that would discourage boys—but an "action figure." G.I. Joe had two other defining characteristics—a scar on his right cheek and an inverted thumbnail which Hasbro used to protect their creation from copyright infringement.

Four G.I. Joe characters (soldier, sailor, pilot, and marine) were released in 1964 and were a smash hit with consumers, who purchased two million figures in the first year. In addition to realistic cloth uniforms, kids could collect a dizzying array of more than seventy-five accessories, including weapons, equipment, and vehicles.

Within two years, G.I. Joe accounted for more than 60 percent of Hasbro's profits, and it appeared that Barbie had met her

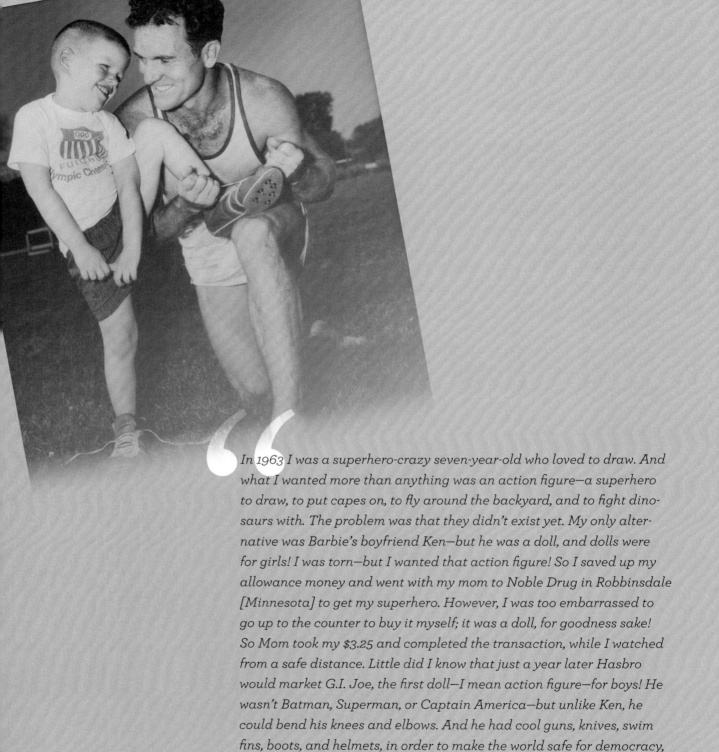

"In 1963 I was a superhero-crazy seven-year-old who loved to draw. And what I wanted more than anything was an action figure—a superhero to draw, to put capes on, to fly around the backyard, and to fight dinosaurs with. The problem was that they didn't exist yet. My only alternative was Barbie's boyfriend Ken—but he was a doll, and dolls were for girls! I was torn—but I wanted that action figure! So I saved up my allowance money and went with my mom to Noble Drug in Robbinsdale [Minnesota] to get my superhero. However, I was too embarrassed to go up to the counter to buy it myself; it was a doll, for goodness sake! So Mom took my $3.25 and completed the transaction, while I watched from a safe distance. Little did I know that just a year later Hasbro would market G.I. Joe, the first doll—I mean action figure—for boys! He wasn't Batman, Superman, or Captain America—but unlike Ken, he could bend his knees and elbows. And he had cool guns, knives, swim fins, boots, and helmets, in order to make the world safe for democracy, and dolls safe for boys everywhere!

GARY FRANK MILLER, b. 1956, instructional designer

match. Yet by the late 1960s a Vietnam War–weary America had become disenchanted with military culture, and Hasbro decided to put G.I. Joe on furlough. The figure returned for duty in the 1970s sporting "life-like" hair and beard, a menacing "Kung-fu grip," "eagle eye" vision, and a new civilian occupation: Adventurer. Despite this transformation, Hasbro curtailed its production of G.I. Joe in 1978, but resurrected the toy in 1982 in a 3¾-inch format based on the tremendous success of similar-sized *Star Wars* figures. Dubbed "G.I. Joe: A Real American Hero," this new lineup consisted of a team of individual characters assembled to combat an evil terrorist organization named Cobra. In recent years, the twelve-inch G.I. Joe has reappeared both as part of the Real American Hero toy line and an anniversary series based on the 1960s figures.

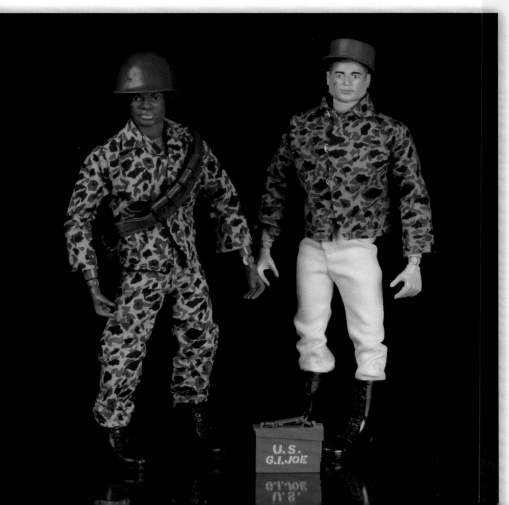

The only thing I wanted at Christmas was G.I. Joe

For a long time during my early childhood, the only thing I wanted at Christmas was G.I. Joe. One Christmas my aunt searched the entire state of New York and probably most of the remainder of the country looking for the Adventure Team Headquarters. She eventually called Hasbro directly. Hasbro actually found two of them in their warehouse and shipped them to her just barely in time for Christmas. One for me and one for my cousin. My Christmas was complete! My late aunt was terrific! Her husband, my uncle, was a real American Hero, a G.I. Joe assigned to the 45th Infantry Division. He was killed in action in 1944 by a German mortar attack at the Battle of Monte Casino in Italy. Having no children of her own, my aunt spoiled me and my other siblings. ALL of my childhood G.I. Joes were gifts from her and that is why they have such a special place in my heart.
MARK WRIGHT, b. 1962, rocket scientist

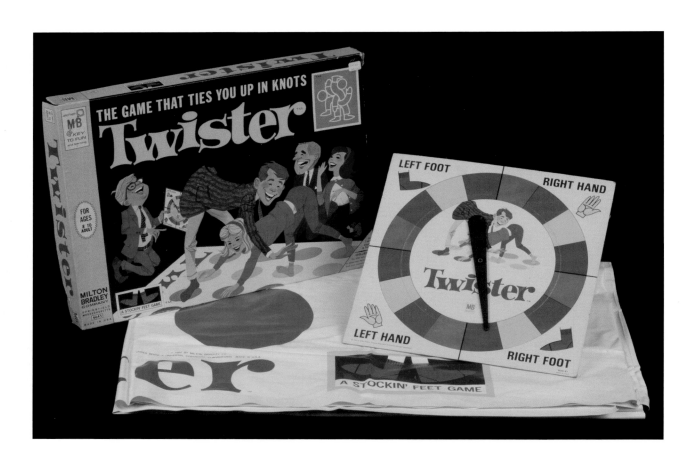

Twister
Milton Bradley Company
1966

Twister

"Sex in a box." That's how Twister's critics labeled the ground-breaking game that, for the first time, placed players of the opposite sex in close—and often provocative—contact with one another. Introduced in 1966 as the nation began to feel a loosening of the moral constrictions of the 1950s, Twister was the right game at the right time. From almost innocuous beginnings it spread like wildfire to become "Game of the Year" in 1967 and was rivaled only by the Hula-Hoop as America's biggest fad toy of the decade.

"The game that ties you up in knots" had an unlikely start in 1965 as a back-to-school shoe promotional display created by St. Paul–based ad man Reyn Guyer. Working with a colored polka dot mat to highlight kids' shoes, Guyer realized the potential of making the mat into a game where people became active pieces. Calling it King's Footsie, Guyer teamed up with game designers Charles F. Foley and Neil Rabens, who further refined the idea and licensed it to Milton Bradley under the name Pretzel. Milton Bradley liked the game—which uses a spinner to direct players to place their hands and feet on different colored circles on a mat without falling over in a heap—but not the name, and renamed it Twister.

Initial sales of Twister were lackluster. Some retailers were perplexed by it, while others, like department store giant Sears, thought the game was too suggestive and refused to carry it. But when the American public caught a glimpse of Johnny Carson and Hungarian-born actress Eva Gabor humorously entangled as they played the game on the *Tonight Show* on May 3, 1966, sales skyrocketed. Twister quickly made its way into suburban house parties and college campuses across the country, and more than three million copies were sold over the next year.

It's estimated that over 65 million people have played

T.M.

Twister since its introduction in 1966. Why the great success? Reyn Guyer, who would later invent another landmark toy called the NERF ball, claimed it was, in part, timing. "Ideas that become iconic tend to break rules or norms. Twister broke the rules in a social setting. People had not up to that point been granted the possibility of being that close and enjoying it in a group setting." The rules had indeed been broken: a mantra for Twister . . . and the '60s.

Twister developers Charles Foley and Neil Rabens demonstrate the game in Minnesota, 1966

Patenting "Right hand, yellow; Left foot, green"

Although Reyn Guyer developed the initial concept for Twister, it was Charles Foley and Neil Rabens who would be granted a patent for the game in 1969. When asked by the U.S. Patent Office what mechanical parts they would be patenting, the inventors responded that the players would serve as the parts. Foley even traveled to Washington, DC, to demonstrate the game for patent officials. Their application, entitled "Apparatus for Playing a Game Wherein the Players Constitute the Game Pieces," must have befuddled even the most seasoned government bureaucrats with a process that required each player to possess "a considerable degree of skill, timing, and coordinated muscular control, all in order successfully to make such body movements as to entwine his body in a pretzel-like manner around the body of an opponent."

Spirograph
Kenner Products
1967

Spirograph

Like many popular toys, the Spirograph didn't always live up to the hype. Sometimes a pen would malfunction, ruining an intricate design with an unsightly blob of ink. Sometimes one false move would cause a pen to slip out of its track. Worst of all, you could become distracted halfway through a drawing and lose your place in the instructions.

But when it worked, the results were magical. "A simple and fascinating way to DRAW a million marvelous patterns," according to a tag line on the original box, the Spirograph set consisted of eighteen wheels, two rings, and two racks, all made of transparent plastic and fitted into a special storage tray; four ballpoint pens (red, green, blue, and black); a cardboard base and pack of paper; a set of pins; and a full-color illustrated pattern book. You could follow the instructions and replicate the designs in the pattern book, or go freestyle and create your own.

Bruno Abakanowicz, a Polish mathematician and engineer, invented the spirograph in the late nineteenth century as a means of calculating an area defined by curves. There were early drawing toys based on Abakanowicz's principles, including the Marvelous Wondergraph of 1908, which—at least according to the illustration on its box—seemed more like a mechanical-drawing instrument than a toy. Hoot-Nanny, the Magic Designer, enjoyed some popularity in the 1930s, and the Dizzy Doodler premiered in 1949. But nothing enjoyed the success of the Spirograph.

The toy known worldwide today was invented by Denys Fisher, a British mechanical engineer who worked for his family business, King Fisher Engineering. It began as an idea for a pattern drawing machine for industrial use. But by the time Fisher fully realized his creation, his family members convinced him that the intricate, colorful designs he produced could be

It made me think I could draw

The Spirograph was my absolute favorite toy and my folks must have bought me at least three of them. (Those little plastic teeth on the wheels wore out eventually!) I loved the Spirograph because it made me think I could draw, and the most intricate designs were usually the most difficult to do and required the most patience. I was never a patient sort of kid (nor am I as an adult), but the Spirograph required, and taught, patience. I spent hours creating intricate designs that my folks proudly displayed on the refrigerator. I think I finally outgrew it in my early teens. However, I'm planning on buying one for my grandniece, hoping she gets as much fun out of it as I did.

JACKIE LAVAQUE,
b. 1963, paralegal

marketed as a toy. The Denys Fisher Toys Group, with twelve employees, was formed in 1965.

Two years later, Kenner introduced his toy in the United States, where it was an instant hit. "WARNING—HIGHLY CONTAGIOUS—SPIROMANIA AFFECTS TOTS TO TEENS," read a 1969 advertisement. "Only three known cures—be prepared." Once the Spirograph had a foothold in the marketplace, Kenner introduced the "known cures" touted in this ad. The Super Spirograph ("the answer to a Spirofanatic's dreams") included an array of curved and straight pieces that could be joined to make increasingly intricate designs. The Spirotot came with chunky, colored rings designed for small hands.

YOU CAN MAKE THOUSANDS OF PROFESSIONAL QUALITY DESIGNS

IT'S EASY!

COMPLETE WITH
■ COLORED PENS
■ RING GEAR
■ DESIGN GEARS
■ WORK BOARD
■ HOLDER PINS
■ INSTRUCTIONS

DESIGN-O-MARX

Part of the Spirograph's success no doubt lay in the aura of "educational toy" that surrounded it. Adults could feel good about purchasing a toy "based on mathematical principles and precision engineered," as it was described in the instruction book (or was it a technical manual?) packaged with the Spirograph. But the real genius behind Fisher's creation? It leveled the playing field. "A young child or an adult can draw beautiful designs at once," declared the instruction book. The writer might have added, "even if said child or adult has no apparent artistic talent." Follow the instructions, work slowly and methodically, and yes, you—even if you can't tell one end of a paintbrush from the other—can create a masterpiece.

Other toy makers were anxious to claim their share of spiromania. None other than the legendary Louis Marx, whom *Time* magazine dubbed "America's toy king and café-society Santa" in 1955, introduced one such product. The Design-O-Marx box featured a boy and girl playing with their knock-off version, seemingly as contentedly as their counterparts on the Spirograph box.

Dr. Doolittle See 'n Say

Mattel, Inc.

1967

See 'n Say

One doesn't ordinarily use the word "loquacious" when describing a toy. After all, they're inanimate objects. But talking toys have been around since 1890, when Thomas Edison hollowed out a doll body and embedded a miniature phonograph with a wax cylinder that played up to twelve nursery rhymes, including "Mary Had a Little Lamb" and "Jack and Jill." Mattel's Chatty Cathy doll, released in 1960, also used a small, low-fidelity phonograph to spout out eleven prerecorded phrases, such as "I love you" and "Give me a kiss," with the pull of a string. That pull-string, which became known in the toy business as the "Chatty-Ring," and the simple phonographic recording process pioneered by Edison were repurposed by Mattel in 1965 to create a wildly successful educational toy called the See 'n Say.

The See 'n Say was Mattel's entrée into educational toys for preschoolers, a market that had been dominated by Play-skool for three decades. Tactile toys such as blocks, bead counters, and the ever-popular Lincoln Logs developed concentration and hand-eye coordination, but an audio educational toy to teach children about language and sounds was a novel concept. The Farmer Says See 'n Say was the first to be introduced and made eleven animal sounds when the pointer (a miniature farmer character) was directed at a corresponding animal image on the face of the toy. Pull the string and out comes, "The cow says, Moooo!" For many youngsters, it was the first time hearing a cow, a duck, or a sheep, and the experience was magical.

Best of all, the See 'n Say didn't require batteries, as the phonographic disk containing the audio track was activated by the pull-string. The Farmer Says See 'n Say was so successful that Mattel introduced a host of other versions, including the Bee Says, which recited letters of the alphabet; the Mister Sound Says, which replicated city sounds; and Mister Music Says, which made musical instrument sounds. By the 1970s, entertainment editions featuring Disney characters and other children's favorites like Dr. Doolittle had infiltrated the See 'n Say lineup along with battery-operated models, and by the 1990s the disk recordings had been replaced by sound tracks stored on computer chips. Although the technology has changed and the See 'n Say is now sold by Mattel subsidiary Fisher-Price, the Farmer Says edition is still going strong, encouraging kids the world over to say "Moooo!"

"Hear the Story! Read the Story!"

In 1967 Mattel introduced the See 'n Say Talking Storybooks with the slogan "Hear the Story! Read the Story!" Kids could turn to a scene in the book — made up of washable, tear-proof pages — then aim the pointer and pull the string to listen to Mother Goose recite a nursery rhyme or to hear the whir of a helicopter or the roar of a circus lion.

Big Wheel
Louis Marx & Company
1969

Big Wheel

Is it just a happy coincidence that the Big Wheel and the film *Easy Rider*—that homage to independence, individuality, and Harleys—both debuted in 1969? For any kid who rode a Big Wheel in the 1970s, the sheer exhilaration of flying down a sidewalk or driveway just inches from the pavement was akin to Peter Fonda's "Wyatt" cruising the open road on his "Captain America" chopper. Pick up some more speed, then hit the hand brake and pull the front wheel and you could also land some awesome 360-degree spins. The Big Wheel didn't just improve on the tricycle; it transformed it from Mom's sensible Chevy on a milk run to a Formula One on an Indy 500 victory lap.

So what made the Big Wheel such a big deal? Tricycles had been around since the late 1700s, but they were largely a novelty until the late nineteenth century, when a trike craze swept England and then the United States. Early versions made of wood or steel perched the rider above the front wheel, which slowed the bike down and made it less stable in tight turns. In the 1960s Ray Lohr, lead designer for Louis Marx & Company, remembered as a kid inverting the frame on his trike and pedaling over the back axle. In fact, a number of manufacturers made tricycles with inverted frames during the Depression in order to increase the toy's longevity.

Lohr used this concept to design the Big Wheel, which included an adjustable seat, a hand brake, and an oversized front drive wheel that placed the rider in a low, reclining position. The toy was constructed of molded plastic, which reduced weight and increased speed and comfort when riding over rough surfaces. Most notably, the front wheel sported a molded tread that made a distinctive scraping sound on pavement, announcing the rider's arrival to racing friends and foes alike. The Big Wheel was a tremendous success, bolstered in part by a claim from

" *I loved the power*

So many of my friends had a Big Wheel. Man, were those machines tricked out! Flags flappin' and wheels clackin' as kids flew down their driveways and on the street where we lived. I was lucky enough to get one in the mid-'70s, but to my surprise my Big Wheel did not make the clacking noise like those of my friends. Many years later my dad admitted that he neglected to install the clackers when he assembled my Big Wheel. My brother and I eventually made our own noise with our Big Wheels. Our driveway had a moderate slope that seemed terrifying in those days, but really is not all that steep. We'd race down the driveway and spin out in the street. To do so we'd lock our legs to freeze the pedals and the big wheel itself. We did that often enough the same way that we wore flat spots on the plastic big wheel and it would "ker-klunk" as we rode along. I guess we got the noisemaker in spite of my dad's effort to limit extraneous noise!

DAVID M. GRABITSKE, b. 1970, outreach services manager

the Consumer Product Safety Commission that it was actually safer than a conventional tricycle because of its low rider profile. Throughout the 1970s there were spin-offs like the Hot Cycle and successors like the Green Machine—which steered from the back using levers rather than handlebars—and by the end of the decade, Big Wheel had become a household name. With a first taste of autonomy thanks to the Big Wheel, many boomer kids would quickly learn to appreciate the freedom mobility could bring. Or as Wyatt exclaimed in *Easy Rider*, "I'm hip about time, but I just gotta go."

Marx capitalized on the success of the Big Wheel and released the Green Machine in 1975. Designed for older kids, the machine was steered by control sticks connected to the rear axle and featured the same road-hugging qualities of its predecessor.

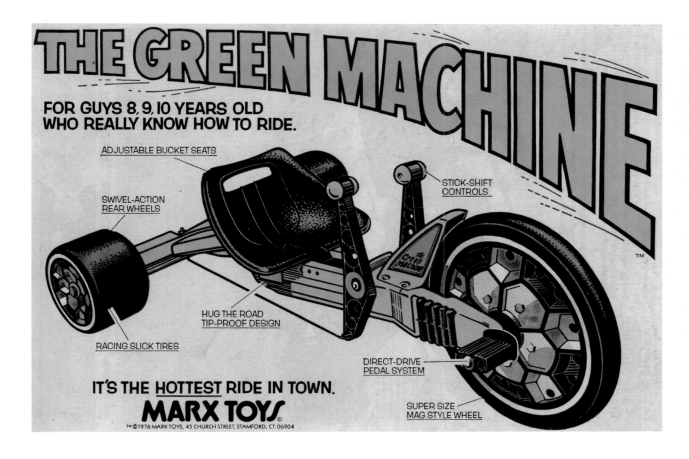

THE GREEN MACHINE

FOR GUYS 8, 9, 10 YEARS OLD
WHO REALLY KNOW HOW TO RIDE.

ADJUSTABLE BUCKET SEATS

SWIVEL-ACTION
REAR WHEELS

STICK-SHIFT
CONTROLS

HUG THE ROAD
TIP-PROOF DESIGN

RACING SLICK TIRES

DIRECT-DRIVE
PEDAL SYSTEM

SUPER SIZE
MAG STYLE WHEEL

IT'S THE **HOTTEST** RIDE IN TOWN.
MARX TOYS

™©1976 MARX TOYS, 45 CHURCH STREET, STAMFORD, CT. 06904

Julia doll
Mattel, Inc.
1968

Julia Doll

On September 17, 1968, NBC broadcast the first of eighty-six episodes of the sitcom *Julia,* starring Diahann Carroll as a widowed single mother employed as a nurse. It was not the first television show to feature an African American woman as the lead: Ethel Waters had starred in *Beulah* in the early 1950s. But the timing of *Julia*'s debut, less than six months after the assassination of Rev. Martin Luther King Jr. and in a year marked by violent protests and civil unrest, almost guaranteed that it would be the subject of fierce debate. Critics attacked its depiction of Julia and her son living in a suburban setting, "a far, far cry from the bitter realities of Negro life in the urban ghetto," as Robert Lewis Shayon wrote in the *Saturday Review*. Others took a more measured view. "Since the networks have had a rash of shows dealing with the nation's racial problems," offered a writer for *Ebony* magazine, "the light-hearted *Julia* provides welcome relief, if, indeed, relief is even acceptable in these troubled times."

With television-related toys and games popular in the late '60s, it's not surprising that Mattel introduced a Julia doll shortly after the sitcom's early episodes began earning favorable ratings. Manufactured with a Barbie body and a Christie head, Julia was sold in a nurse's uniform. Other outfits were available, and eventually both Twist 'n Turn and Talking Julia dolls were introduced.

The same mixed reviews aimed at *Julia,* from an inaccurate portrayal to a step in the right direction, could be applied to her namesake doll. The history of African American dolls is complicated, but one clear note rings through—over time many dolls characterized as "black" were made from the same molds as "white" dolls and simply produced in a different shade. Meanwhile, several toy makers and designers took pains to model African American dolls with distinct, accurate features. Dolls in

At least a hint that the world is a diverse place

I had a Julia doll! I loved her. I think she and Skipper were the only Barbie dolls I had. I liked her because I could watch her on TV, too. Also, in the almost entirely white suburb in which I was raised, my parents were so happy that popular culture of the '70s offered at least a hint that the world is a diverse place.

ELIZABETH OLSON, b. 1965, chief financial officer

the Barbie line did have slightly varied features based on their ethnicity but were not markedly different from each other.

Demand for African American dolls has always existed, and stories of young girls longing to see themselves reflected in their toys abound. Debra Britt, who with her sisters founded the National Black Doll Museum in Mansfield, Massachusetts, carried a vinyl white Baby Bye-Lo doll in the 1950s. "I didn't have a lot of self-esteem with it," Britt recalled for *Collectors Weekly*. "I had big issues because I was black and fat, and kids were teasing me. And I had to ride a bus with nobody on it. When I would get to school, the other kids shook my bus every day and called me names." If school didn't offer friends who looked like her, wouldn't a young girl find solace in a doll who did, one who affirmed her sense of worth when the rest of the world didn't?

In the same 1968 issue of *Ebony* that featured Diahann Carroll as Julia on its cover, an article titled "The Advent of Soul Toys" described an "ethnically correct" line of dolls designed by African American artist Annuel McBurrows, "and the result is absolutely delightful." The article shed light on "a great untapped market for black-oriented toys. That an 'integrated' toy industry may help Negro children develop a sense of identity and racial pride is a fringe concern to businessmen but of major importance to parents sensitive to positive black consciousness."

Elizabeth Olson at center

Of the many African American dolls produced in the '50s, '60s, and '70s, Sara Lee stands out as a symbol of one woman's determination. In 1949 Florida business owner and activist Sara Lee Creech began her quest to produce a doll that would promote positive images of African Americans for children of all races. She approached sculptor Sheila Burlingame to create the doll head and solicited a letter of support from former first lady Eleanor Roosevelt, who described the doll as "a lesson in equality for little children." Creech then enlisted the help of black leaders, including Ralph Bunche and Mary McLeod Bethune, in convincing Ideal Toy Company to manufacture the doll.

Sara Lee received many positive reviews when she made her 1951 appearance. Author Zora Neale Hurston wrote, "They will surely meet a long-felt need among us. It is a magnificently constructive thing . . . for the whole of America, as well as for Negro children." Sara Lee was manufactured by Ideal for only two years, in part because the vinyl used in her construction was easily cracked, faded, and leached dye onto the doll's clothing. It wasn't until 1968 that another mass-marketed African American doll — Barbie's friend Christie — would become a commercial success. But Sara Lee Creech, who continued to promote interracial harmony through the establishment of daycare centers for migrant workers in the 1950s and 1960s, had the satisfaction of knowing that one woman — and one toy — can make a real difference.

Sara Lee doll
Ideal Toy Company
1951–53

The 1970s

Robert J. Smith III

More than any recent decade, the 1970s has a bad rap. Our collective memory renders the '70s more punch line than pivotal—an era of bad music, bad hair, and bad clothing. By the close of the decade, many Americans believed that our politicians, our principles, and our polyester had failed us. Perhaps it was inevitable that the '70s would take a historical backseat to its unruly older sibling, the 1960s, with its protests, iconic music festivals, and seemingly radical breaks with the past. One historian summed up our memory of the decade: like the Pet Rock popular at the time, the 1970s was a period when nothing happened—nothing good, at least. With a closer look, however, the 1970s appears more like a major turning point than a mere bump in the road. In many ways, the '70s gave us the country we live in today.

Disco might be the perfect metaphor for the decade, which, like Tony Manero, *Saturday Night Fever*'s working-class hero, was fraught with conflict and contradiction. The genre, epitomized by flamboyant clothing, swiveling hips, and thumping beats, reached its peak during the '70s and, following the social movements of the 1960s, brought new visibility to African Amer-

1970
Members of the growing environmental movement celebrate Earth Day for the first time.

1971
The United States discontinues its trade embargo on goods from China.

icans, Latinos, and gays in popular culture. However, by the close of the '70s, the dance floor democracy of disco was the butt of many jokes, a symbol of a decadent culture, and the target of a passionate backlash. Disco's final blow was dealt at the infamous 1979 Disco Demolition Night at Chicago's Comiskey Park, when more than 70,000 people gathered, armed with anti-disco signs and chants of "Disco Sucks!" to watch the destruction of thousands of the maligned genre's records. The night ended in rioting and dozens of injuries. What some called progress, others called radicalism. Many resented that traditional values were falling away, while others popularized new ways of being. It may have been enough to convince even Tony Manero to turn in his dancing shoes.

If we put down our drinks, step off the dance floor, and peer into American living rooms, we might instead remember the '70s through the eyes of the coarse working-class stiff Archie Bunker or the upwardly mobile but unrefined George Jefferson. *All in the Family,* or simply "Archie" to many of its viewers, was the most-watched show on television for the first half of the decade. For nine seasons, Archie, surrounded by his wife Edith, daughter Gloria, and son-in-law Mike, spared no one with his biting and bigoted criticism of how the post-'60s world was changing. In the long-running spin-off *The Jeffersons,* George and Louise leave their neighbors Archie and Edith in working-class Queens, "movin' on up" to urban affluence in Manhattan, symbols of a

1972

Public health officials shut down the notorious forty-year Tuskegee syphilis experiment in which rural African American men were left untreated for syphilis to study its effects.

1973

The U.S. Supreme Court rules in *Roe v. Wade* that women have the right to seek abortion.

1974

President Richard M. Nixon resigns from office to avoid his likely impeachment. His successor, President Gerald R. Ford, later pardons Nixon of any crimes related to the Watergate scandal.

growing black middle class and the partial success of the civil rights movement. The transition isn't always easy for the Jeffersons, as they confront racial discrimination even while climbing the economic ladder.

Regardless of political affiliation, millions tuned in each week to laugh at—or with—Archie and George grappling with the changing world around them as the 1970s marched on: through the American War in Vietnam, the oil crisis, Watergate, Nixon's resignation, the mainstreaming of environmentalism, mass labor strikes, women's liberation, Black Power, the American Indian Movement, the growing power of the religious right, the fall of the Equal Rights Amendment, "stagflation," the shootings at Kent State, *Roe v. Wade,* and accelerated globalization, just to name a few of the decade's landmarks. Far from being an era when time stood still, the 1970s pushed us into the future in which we live today. The morass at Comiskey and the strivings of Archie, George, and their families capture the struggles of a nation grappling with epochal social change and celebrating the joys of stayin' alive.

1975
Comedian George Carlin hosts the first episode of *Saturday Night Live*, NBC's long-running sketch comedy show.

1976
Apple Computer Company is founded by Steve Jobs and Steve Wozniak.

For Further Reading

Jefferson R. Cowie, *Stayin' Alive: The 1970s and the Last Days of the Working Class*

Alice Echols, *Hot Stuff: Disco and the Remaking of American Culture*

Gillian Frank, "Discophobia: Antigay Prejudice and the 1979 Backlash against Disco," *Journal of the History of Sexuality*, May 2007

Bruce J. Schulman, *The Seventies: The Great Shift in American Culture, Society, and Politics*

Robert O. Self, *All in the Family: The Realignment of American Democracy Since the 1960s*

1977

San Francisco elects Harvey Milk as a city supervisor, making him the first openly gay member of the supervisory board, a first for a large U.S. city.

1978

The Women's Army Corps, founded during World War II, is abolished and women are integrated into the regular U.S. Army.

1979

McDonald's introduces its fast-food staple the Happy Meal. A toy is included in each box.

Uno Deluxe Edition

International Games, Inc.

1978

Uno

Merle Robbins took his hobby seriously. An avid card game enthusiast, Robbins was playing Crazy Eights with his son Ray in 1970 when the pair got into a spat about the rules of the game. In the course of resolving the dispute, the barber from Reading, Ohio, devised a new card game he called Uno. Essentially a twist on Crazy Eights, the objective of the game is to get rid of your cards as quickly as possible, with the winner being the first player with zero cards left in his hand. When players have one card left, they must yell "Uno!" or, if they forget, draw two more cards from the deck. Once a player has no cards left, the hand is over and points are scored.

Uno became a favorite in the Robbins home, with the original decks being designed and made on the dining room table. As Uno grew in popularity with friends and family, Robbins decided to have the game manufactured. His family pooled $10,000 to have five thousand games printed, which Robbins then sold out of his barbershop. In 1971 Robbins was contacted by Robert Tezak, a funeral home owner in Joliet, Illinois, about purchasing the rights to the game. Robbins agreed to a payment of $50,000 plus royalties, and Tezak, along with his brother-in-law Ed Akeman and other partners, started International Games, Inc., to market what would be dubbed "America's most popular family card game."

Uno got off to a slow start, selling only about five thousand units in its first year, mostly by word of mouth. Then, in 1978 K-Mart discount department stores arranged to carry the game nationally and sales took off. Since then, more than 150 million copies have been sold worldwide, and it's estimated that 80 percent of America's game-playing households have gathered around the Uno deck at some time or another.

When I won my first game and shouted "Uno," I was hooked

From the first time I saw it I was intrigued. My first Uno game was when I was a kid. It was a Christmas gift and one that I to this day feel was the best gift ever. When I opened the deck, read the directions, explained them to my family, and then all my family present at Christmas sat down to play, it was magical. It was fun, loud, and exciting. When I won my first game and shouted "Uno," I was hooked. After that we played often. There was laughter, fun, and teasing. I took my Uno game wherever I could and played with whoever was willing. As the years went on I still played but not as often. In college I bought a new Uno deck so I could have some fun on those nights I had night duty as an RA for my college. And I found others who loved the game. During my night duty I would put out the word that an Uno game was on. People would come and we would have some cutthroat games. Some with as high as twenty people with others waiting to take the place of the losers. It was a fun rotation of people to match Uno wits with. It was a great time.

TAIGE CRENSHAW, author

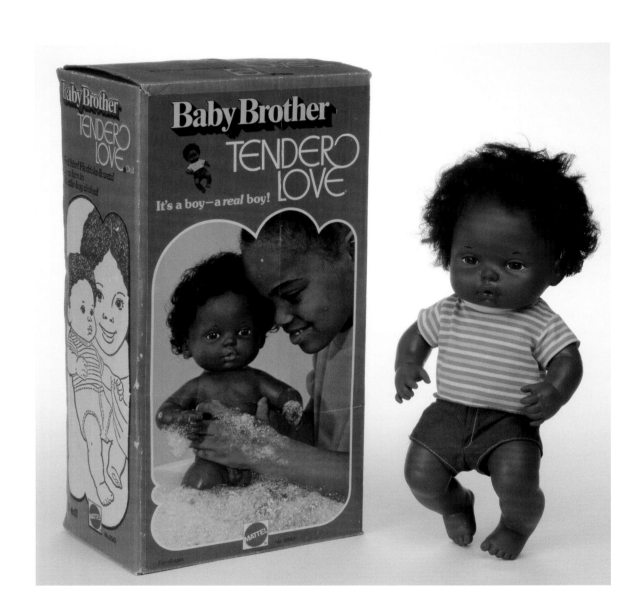

Baby Brother Tender Love
Mattel, Inc.
1975

Baby Tender Love

Living in the shadow of Barbie isn't easy. Mattel's bestseller dominated the doll market throughout the 1960s, sending company designers scrambling to come up with something new and unique. Talking dolls were a fixture at Mattel in the 1960s, with Chatty Cathy (the second-best-selling doll of the decade), talking members of the Barbie clan, and Baby Teenie Talk. Ideal's Betsy Wetsy, one of the most popular dolls of the baby boom era, had made its mark in the industry as a drink-and-wet figure, and Mattel was eager to best her. Mattel's strategy was to manufacture a multifaceted line of dolls that would satisfy a growing consumer demand for realism and serve as a source of encouragement and edification for children in their prospective roles as parents.

In 1969 the toy maker introduced the Baby Tender Love series, featuring male and female Caucasian and African American dolls with a lifelike vinyl skin called Dublon. Although many had non-posable bodies, the Living Baby Tender Love had jointed limbs, so it could, in the words of a 1971 Sears Christmas catalog, "tumble over like a real baby." The nineteen-inch-tall Living doll also came in a talking version, with phrases like "Kiss Baby," "Go bye-bye," and "Night-night." And yes, it was a drink-and-wet doll as well. In 1972 a Tearful Baby Tender Love was released, followed by a Bless You model in 1974 that sneezed when its tummy was squeezed. Dolls that could pose, talk, drink, wet, cry, and sneeze—all with cuddly skin as soft as a baby's: one would think Mattel's designers had achieved their goal. But there was one more feature to offer, and it would change the doll industry forever.

Baby Brother Tender Love, Mattel's first anatomically correct male doll, came discreetly packaged with a disclosure so as not to startle parents or children. Mattel had to rely heavily

A sure sign of the coming revolution

Growing up in a house filled with females, the best way a girl could educate herself about male anatomy was to find a friend who owned Baby Brother Tender Love. Our neighbors had the same problem. They were a family of three sisters, and I was best friends with Lori and Nancy. But between us [we] couldn't locate a single peer who had access to Baby Brother. When news hit that a local department store received a shipment of the anatomically correct male baby doll, we made a date after school to visit the merchant. We found Baby Brother Tender Love on a top shelf in a dark corner of the toy section. The box showed a young girl with a creepy grin fondling the doll as she bathed him. Her hand strategically covered the parts we had come to see. "We're going to have to take him out of the box," I directed. As soon as we pulled the box down we were approached by management. "Is there something I can help you girls with?" the dour matron inquired. Usually in these situations we could count on Nancy to drum up a good story, but she froze in the face of elderly authority. Shy Lori had already escaped to the Garanimals aisle, so she was no help. Thinking quickly, I spat out a fantastic lie, "We need to find a present for our friend's birthday." "Well, you girls need to find a present in a different aisle. You cannot buy this doll without your parents' permission." I suppose we must have known what a controversy Baby Brother was causing among prudes everywhere. It was the '70s. There was fear that Free Love and drugs might trickle into Small Town Minnesota at any second, and these penis dolls were a sure sign of the coming revolution.

PATRICE M. JOHNSON, b. 1966, author and cooking instructor

on a print campaign aimed at mothers rather than kids, since television codes would not even permit showing a doll's bare bottom. Although some were surprised by the doll, it was not Mattel's first foray into "plastic imitates life." In 1975 the toy maker had debuted Growing Up Skipper, which allowed Barbie's little sister to extend her torso and grow her bust with a twist of her arm. Interestingly enough, Baby Brother was produced at the request of doll buyers, although there apparently was no such demand for an anatomically correct baby sister. Nevertheless, the tide had decidedly turned, reflecting a trend toward a more candid toy culture.

Baby Brother

MATTEL

TENDER LOVE DOLL

1 Fill the baby bottle ½ full with water.

2 Feed your BABY BROTHER TENDER LOVE with his bottle until he wets.

PRESS BOTTLE AGAINST LIPS

3 Hold the baby in your lap. Squeeze in the CENTER of his tummy until he wets.

IMPORTANT: When you give your new doll a bath, treat him just like a real baby. Never put his head under water.

If his hair gets wet or soapy, make sure it is rinsed thoroughly and combed while wet. This will keep his hair neat.

©MATTEL, Inc. 1975, Hawthorne, California 90250. Printed in U.S.A. All Rights Reserved.

9524-00920A

Play Family Castle
Fisher-Price Toys
1974

Play Family Castle

Harnessing the power of imagination is perhaps the greatest gift a toy can give to a young child. And sometimes that gift can come from the simplest of designs, devoid of flashing lights, whirring noises, or even multiple moving parts. Sometimes less is more because it enables a child to envision the possibilities without distraction or manipulation. Fisher-Price's Play Family figures, better known today as "Little People," are a classic case in point. Introduced in 1959, these unpretentious characters, constructed of wooden pegs clad in lithographed "clothing," were originally conceived as adornment to the company's Safety School Bus toy. The first "Play Family" of figures was introduced the following year with the Nifty Station Wagon. The figures proved so popular with children that they spawned a line of play sets, including an amusement park, farm, house, school, and many more.

The success of the Play Family series was hardly an accident. Established in 1930 by game manufacturer Herman Fisher, retired retailer Irving Price, and toy store owner Helen Schelle, Fisher-Price set a mission to make toys with "intrinsic play value, ingenuity, strong construction, good value for the money, and action." Price's wife, Margaret, a children's author and illustrator, was the creative force behind some of the company's early signature toys, including Granny Doodle, Doctor Doodle, and Snoopy Sniffer. Fisher-Price enjoyed great success in the late 1950s with the introduction of Snap-Lock Beads and the Corn Popper, and it became a beacon in the world of educational toys with the launch of the stacking game Rock-A-Stack in the early 1960s.

In 1961 Fisher-Price established a Play Lab—one of the first facilities of its kind—to observe children's feedback to toys under development. This commitment to empirical testing was

Get on the bus: the Fisher-Price Safety School Bus introduced Play Family figures in 1959. In 1985 the company changed their name to "Little People," as customers called them.

rooted in the company's founding creed that "Children love best the cheerful, friendly toys with amusing action, toys that appeal to their imagination, toys that do something new and surprising and funny. This idea is so simple, it is sometimes overlooked— but if you have forgotten your own younger days, test it out on the nearest children."

The Play Family Castle was launched in 1974 and became one of Fisher-Price's most popular Play Family play sets. Festooned with an elaborate array of trapdoors, dungeons, sliding stairs, a working drawbridge, and dragon chambers, the castle provided abundant play value and opportunity for children to employ their imagination. And what would a castle be without a king, his queen, a prince and princess, knights, and a . . . pink dragon? Perhaps the most compelling features of the castle were the copious nooks and crannies for hiding these figures, including a secret passage under the staircase. Although it was only made for three years (1974–77), the castle proved so popular that it was reissued in 1988 for a new generation of youngsters to enjoy.

Peggy Walter

I really loved that castle

The Christmas when I was five (1974) was when I received my Fisher-Price Castle! It was absolutely perfect! My two brothers and I would construct an entire village out of all the Fisher-Price things we had (barn, house, Main Street, castle) along with other things like Lincoln Logs, Weeble Wobble farm, camper, and marina as well as a Noah's Ark and a McDonalds set . . . we'd use it all for hours especially on rainy or really cold days!

PEG WALTER OLSON, b. 1969, facility services manager

My favorite toy of all time was the Fisher-Price Castle. Stand your prisoner over the trapdoor and he instantly falls down into the dungeon at the bottom of the castle. The dungeon was pretty cool, too. It had a door that could be opened so the prisoner could be released and neat lithographs of a pond outside the door.

KELLY LIPP, b. 1971, disabilities program coordinator

Lil' Chik Bicycle
Schwinn Bicycle Company
1977

Lil' Chik Bicycle

From skateboards to the Beach Boys, West Coast surf culture had begun to infiltrate all facets of American life by the early 1960s. Muscle cars, hot rods, and chopper motorcycles—which had their origins in California—not only inspired a nationwide fascination with drag racing but sparked a revolution in design aesthetics that influenced everything from graphic design to hair styles to fashion. Kustom Kulture, as it became known, captured a fun, lowbrow style that placed an emphasis on individuality and self-expression. The results were always unconventional and more often than not outrageous. Kulture kings like Ed "Big Daddy" Roth, creator of the grotesque hot rod icon Rat Fink, and Kenny "Von Dutch" Howard, originator of the famous "flying eyeball" logo, exemplified the rebellious and irreverent creativity at the core of the movement.

Kustom Kulture made its influence known in the cycling industry in the early '60s, when imaginative young teens in suburban Los Angeles began to modify their bicycles to emulate the lines of Harley Davidson choppers by tricking out twenty-inch bike frames with ape-hanger handlebars and banana seats. Schwinn Bicycle Company designer Al Fritz went to California to check out the bikes, loved what he saw, and returned to Schwinn headquarters in Chicago to devise a prototype. Skeptical executives reluctantly agreed to release the Schwinn Sting-Ray, clad in colors like "Flamboyant Lime" and adorned with butterfly handlebars and a "Solo-Polo" banana seat, in June 1963.

Response to the Sting-Ray was nothing short of extraordinary, and within months of its debut more than 45,000 bikes were sold. With its eccentric looks and wheelie-popping performance, Schwinn had hit a home run with young teens eager to stand out from the crowd. Marketing it as the "Sports Car" bike for kids too young to drive, Schwinn built on the Sting-Ray's suc-

Schwinn **LIL' CHIK** ®

For girls 5 to 7. Compact Schwinn electro-forged frame, chrome plated fenders, and the new flowered saddle with chrome struts. Schwinn tubular rims, 20" x 1¾" front tire, 20" x 1¾" Gripper Slik rear tire, built-in kickstand. Colors: Violet, Campus Green.

J81-7 Lil' Chik $51.95

"It was my Corvette

My bicycles were always blue. My very favorite was a Schwinn Fair Lady coaster bike. Mother wouldn't let me get the hand brakes because she "didn't trust them." Seems she once saw someone squeeze a hand brake and fly over the handlebars, so they were completely off the table. With whitewall tires and stainless steel fenders, it was my Corvette. I had a brief affair with a banana seat bike in the mid-1960s, but I never loved a bike like I did my Fair Lady.
SHERRI GARDNER HOWELL, columnist

"*Around 1970 I was a very proud owner of a Schwinn Classic Sting-Ray. It was a metallic royal blue with matching "banana" seat. As a girl, I had the requisite white basket with flower appliqués. Naturally, my brothers wouldn't be caught dead on my bike. But I spent most of my good-weather days on that bike riding around with my brothers and the neighborhood kids.*
ANN-MARIE AIYAWAR, b. 1961, web merchandiser

cess by introducing after-market accessories like chrome sissy bars and treadless "slick" tires.

In 1964 Schwinn introduced the Fair Lady, a bike for "mother, daughter, or even grandmother," which echoed many features of the Sting-Ray with the addition of a flower-trimmed wicker basket affixed to the handlebars. But what about younger girls who wanted the same quick, responsive handling of a Sting-Ray? A "muscle" bike for little girls? You bet! Launched in 1966, the Schwinn Lil' Chik featured a Sting-Ray-inspired dropped tube frame, short-rise chrome bars, and a flowered polo saddle with chrome struts, all designed for girls aged five to seven years. Advertised as "perfect and petite for growing girls," the Lil' Chik served as Schwinn's junior Sting-Ray offering for emerging female cyclists for more than twenty years.

STING-RAY BIKES FOR GIRLS

Schwinn FAIR LADY®

Perfect for shopping, relaxing, or keeping fit. Trim, low contoured frame that's easy to get on and off. Flower-trimmed basket, new Sting-Ray handlebars, comfortable saddle, chrome plated fenders. Schwinn tubular rims, 20" x 1¾" front tire. 20" x 1¾" Gripper Slik rear tire, built-in kickstand. Colors: Campus Green, White, Violet.

J89-6   Fair Lady, coaster $59.95
J89-4   Fair Lady, 3-speed $69.95

Schwinn SLIK CHIK®

The ladies' middleweight Sting-Ray . . . for the outdoor girl. Sleek sophisticated features include floral-trimmed basket, coordinated color matching saddle, chrome plated fenders, Schwinn tubular rims, new narrow line whitewall front tire and Gripper Slik rear, 20" x 2.125 tire. Built-in rattle free kickstand. Colors: Campus Green, White, Violet.

J90-6   Slik Chik, coaster $66.95
J90-4   Slik Chik, 3-speed $76.95

24

Jarts Missile Game

Jarts Company
Late 1960s–early 1970s

Jarts

It's a simple enough game, with rules similar to horseshoes. Players, individually or in teams, toss plastic darts with weighted ends toward a target on the ground (usually a plastic ring sold as part of the game). You get a point every time you land a dart in a ring. The significance of the game of Jarts lies not in its innovative style of play but in its notorious reputation. If you come across a list of most dangerous toys, odds are good that Jarts—also known as lawn darts, and originally sold with sharp metal tips—are on it.

As long as there have been toys, there have been concerns about their safety. But for centuries kids didn't have many toys, and those they played with were often simple and homemade. In the early 1930s, though, members of the Toy Manufacturers Association, a trade organization, established a Toy Safety Committee. Working with the National Safety Council, the committee began accumulating data on toy injuries and hazards and establishing safety standards. This was a great start—but adherence to the standards was purely voluntary, and definitions of safety varied. That's how the Gilbert U-238 Atomic Energy Lab, complete with four types of uranium ore and including a comic book titled *Dagwood Splits the Atom,* ended up on toy store shelves in time for the 1950 holiday season.

Throughout the 1950s and '60s, alarms were raised about all sorts of toys, from metal figures covered in lead paint to toy arrows and darts to cap guns. Finally, in 1969 President Richard Nixon signed the Child Protection and Toy Safety Act, which authorized the Department of Health, Education and Welfare to test and ban hazardous toys. By the end of 1970 more than three dozen toys had been banned. Two years later the U.S. Consumer Product Safety Commission, an independent agency, took over as the nation's monitor of toy safety.

Which brings us back to Jarts. Some people considered them unsafe from the very start. Others noted that they were a toy made for adults, and that children should only handle them with adult supervision. Over time, the original metal tips on Jarts were replaced with plastic ones, and the safety warnings on their packaging became more strident. Banned by the Consumer Product Safety Commission in 1988, they are still a subject of debate. Whether you love or loathe them, one thing's for certain—Jarts have made an indelible mark on the history of toy safety.

After the Consumer Product Safety Commission voted to ban lawn darts, Commissioner Anne Graham said, "What limited recreational value lawn darts may have is far outweighed by the number of serious injuries and unnecessary deaths . . . There are numerous alternatives to lawn darts, and I would urge adults who have lawn darts to throw them away now."

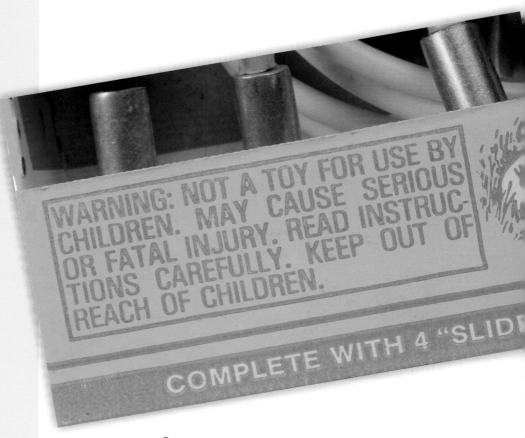

"My parents were always telling us, "Stand back!"

Jarts... This was a fun family game we played in the backyard. Eventually, we took our Jarts up to the cabin, where they still live. My parents were always telling us, "Stand back!" You never knew where the crazy kids were going to throw the soaring missiles, especially if you wanted to scare one of your little siblings!

LISA CRAWFORD ANDERSON, b. 1963, home health training specialist

Johnny Horizon Environmental Test Kit
Parker Brothers
1971

Johnny Horizon Environmental Test Kit

Quick: name a product made by Parker Brothers. Does Monopoly come to mind? Or Clue? How about Trivial Pursuit? In 1971 the company best known for its board games introduced something completely different: a chemistry set designed specifically for environmental testing featuring Johnny Horizon, a square-jawed figure whose slogan was "This is your land—keep it clean."

Johnny Horizon was the brainchild of Boyd Rasmussen, who became director of the Bureau of Land Management in 1966. Rasmussen had spent most of his career with the U.S. Forest Service, where he saw the success of Smokey Bear. From that experience he knew that a memorable symbol could personalize and reinforce the bureau's crusade for a cleaner America. In 1968 Johnny Horizon made his debut as a kindly, middle-aged man dressed in khaki pants, a plaid shirt, and a red jacket, carrying a backpack. As described in the deluge of promotional materials that accompanied his introduction, Johnny was the son of a World War I veteran and descended from the Nez Perce. He was a thoughtful and appreciative user of public lands.

Over the next several years, Johnny's horizons seemed limitless. Academy Award–winning actor and folk singer Burl Ives gave free concerts nationwide to promote his message. In a single month, 23,000 fans signed pledges to reduce litter on public lands. In 1972—the same year Peppermint Patty recalled having a dream about him in a *Peanuts* comic strip—the Department of the Interior adopted Johnny Horizon as the symbol of its Clean Up America campaign. Two years later, President Gerald Ford issued a proclamation declaring "the period September 15 through October 15, 1974, as Johnny Horizon '76 Clean Up America Month . . . to demonstrate the significant results that

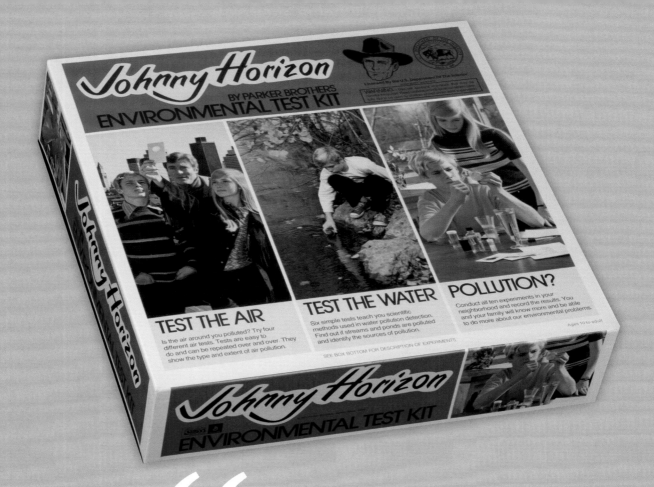

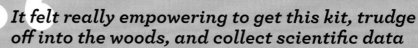

> ## " It felt really empowering to get this kit, trudge off into the woods, and collect scientific data

I grew up in Chester, Virginia, the small town over from Hopewell, the "Chemical Capital of the South." Armed with my Johnny Horizon Test Kit, I was determined to prove that Hopewell was hurting us. I did all of the tests in the kit—suspended particles, wind-blown particles, Coliform, pH, smoke density, nylon deterioration, etc. I did them as a science project and showed that the industrial zone between Hopewell and Chester was crankin' crud into the air and water that was beyond allowable levels (in some tests). Nothing really ever came of it (except an A+ on the project), but it felt really empowering to get this kit, trudge off into the woods, and collect scientific data that actually painted a picture of what was happening in the surrounding area.

GARETH BRANWYN, b. 1958, writer

can be realized when Americans translate their concern into affirmative action."

Parker Brothers provided the new icon with an environmental test kit that included an assortment of glassware, measuring devices, and other scientific equipment, as well as vials of chemicals and a package of Alka-Seltzer. A booklet packaged with the kit described ten experiments for testing air and water. It was an updated version of the chemistry sets so popular in the 1950s and '60s—a kit for kids who recognized that Earth Day (first celebrated in 1970) was something to be taken seriously.

So what became of our environmental hero? "Johnny Horizon has done his job and done it well," said Secretary of the Interior Thomas Kleppe at Johnny's retirement party in 1976. "His life span embraced a time of massive reawakening, of environmental awareness, community action, and citizen participation. People across the land realize that they personally can do much to make our country more livable."

In the post-*Sputnik* era, teachers, scientists, and others advocated for chemistry sets, microscopes, and more to train the next generation of scientists. In the 1960s, astronaut toys were common. It's not surprising, then, that the environmental concerns of the 1970s were reflected in the Johnny Horizon set. Part toys, part tools, science kits are a clear, direct reflection of their times.

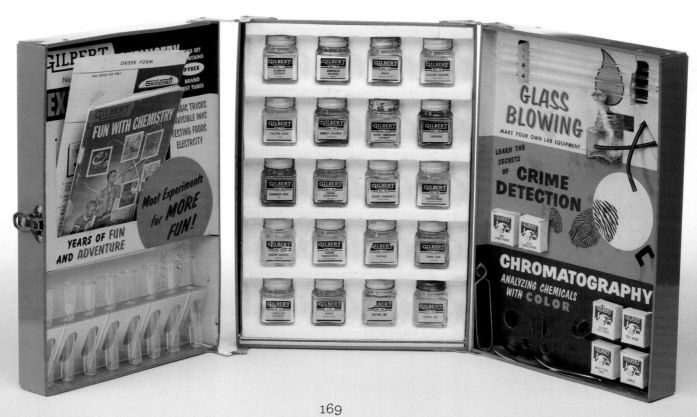

NERF Ball
Parker Brothers
1970

NERF Ball

Reyn Guyer knew a thing or two about toys. After all, the Minneapolis-based inventor had developed the concept for the Milton Bradley blockbuster game of Twister in 1965. In 1968 Guyer was at it again, this time with a game he called Caveman, which entailed using spongy foam "rocks" hurled at rivals to prevent them from stealing play money. Guyer soon realized that the foam balls were more fun to play with than the game, so he re-envisioned the orbs as an accessory to an indoor volleyball set. Milton Bradley passed on the game, but Parker Brothers, makers of Monopoly and Clue, saw promise in the four-inch polyurethane ball and decided to manufacture it as a stand-alone toy.

The NERF ball, marketed as the world's first indoor ball, first appeared in 1970. "Throw it indoors. You can't damage lamps or break windows. You can't hurt babies or old people," the packaging proclaimed. And while the NERF—named after a bumping maneuver used in auto racing to enable a pass—wouldn't take out a window or level Grandma, it was strong enough to topple a vase. Nevertheless, it was a tremendous hit, and more than four million balls were sold in the first year.

The success of the original NERF spawned a larger "Super" NERF ball shortly thereafter, followed by a basketball game dubbed NERFoop, which included a hoop that could be mounted to a wall or door. But NERF's greatest triumph came in 1972 with the debut of the NERF football, the result of a collaboration between football fan John Mattox and Minnesota Vikings kicker Fred Cox. Mattox approached Cox in 1970 with an idea for a kids' kicking game, and Cox suggested a foam football to avert injuries. The pair worked with a plastics manufacturer in the Twin Cities to cast a prototype with a thick rubberized skin that gave the ball a superior trajectory. In fact, Parker Brothers had been tinkering with versions of a NERF football but none had been successful, so when Cox and Mattox approached the toy maker with their rendition a deal was quickly sealed. More economical and pliable than its pigskin predecessor, the NERF football was the perfect companion for the beach or backyard and ultimately became one of the most popular toys of the 1970s.

Packaging label copy extolling NERF's safety around people and breakables

The **Nerf Ball** is made of soft, spongy synthetic foam. The Nerf Ball complies in all respects with the safety requirements of the Child Protection Act of 1966 and the Child Protection and Toy Safety Act of 1969.

Field of Dreams

My brother Mike was [Fran] Tarkenton and I was [Ahmad] Rashad. With a worn-out orange NERF football in my hands, all I could hear were the imaginary fans gasping as I pulled that ball out of the air. We were two brothers taking on our neighborhood friends. Our stadium was the front yard. Our field? Maybe twenty yards, but surely not a hundred yards. We drew those "sandlot" plays in the palm of our hands and executed them over and over again until the grass in our front yard had been transformed into dirt. We drove the Vikings down the field on touchdown drives, until Mom said, "Wash up boys, it's supper time." Where does time go?

JEFF HAGE, newspaper editor

I played with NERF basketball for hours and hours. I was the entire 1970 Knicks team, playing against imaginary foes. I had the hoop hung on my bedroom door and would drive my parents nuts.

SCOTT DESMIT, journalist

McDonald's Familiar Places play set
Playskool, Inc.
1974

McDonald's Familiar Places Play Set

Times had changed. When Playskool introduced its "Familiar Places" line of play sets in the 1970s, the company once known for its sturdy, no-frills wooden trucks, tools, and trains was capturing kids' attention with brightly colored cloth dolls named Dressy Bessy and Dapper Dan, adorable plastic Weebles with egg-shaped bases (remember the tagline "Weebles wobble, but they don't fall down"?), and the Sit 'n Spin, a riding toy that made kids dizzy with excitement. And the company that had once pitched its advertisements to adults who read *Parents* magazine, *Redbook,* and *Psychology Today* was now aiming straight for children through television ads on *Captain Kangaroo*.

The cynical among us might say that with the introduction of these 1970s toys, along with the other "Familiar Places" sets—a Holiday Inn and a Texaco gas station—Playskool had lost sight of its original purpose as a manufacturer of educational toys. After all, in 1968 Playskool had been purchased by Milton Bradley, the company that produced such intellectually rich fare as Chutes and Ladders, Candyland, and Twister.

But consider historian Gary Cross's insight about the 1970s, from his book *Kids' Stuff: Toys and the Changing World of American Childhood:* "The erector sets and baby dolls that had trained children to assume adult roles made less sense to parents who no longer knew what to train their children to become." While kids were loading up their square-headed Playskool avatars with burgers, fries, and shakes, their elders were glued to their television sets, watching their president resign his duties. Following the 1973 oil crisis inflation had soared, and with it, unemployment. Role-playing as a fast-food clerk? Maybe not such a bad idea.

The nature of children's education had changed since Playskool's wooden-toy heyday as well. On November 10, 1969, *Sesame Street* premiered. For the generation raised on learning with Bert, Ernie, Big Bird, and Oscar the Grouch, education meant a fun, fast-paced mix of animation, skits, musical numbers, and snarky, topical humor. Through *Free to Be . . . You and Me,* a 1972 book and, two years later, an ABC Afterschool Special of the same name, children learned that preparing for adult life was, well . . . complicated. The world was changing fast, and through the predictability of drive-thru service and a set of golden arches, Playskool gave children the opportunity for some simple, reassuring play time.

Putting them in the tray return was the best

It was like a scale model of our local McDonald's in Inver Grove Heights, Minnesota. I was impressed that the tile decal in the interior was an exact match of the basket-weave pattern of the tile at the restaurant (apparently patterns in material culture were already important to me). The figures "carried" the trays very unnaturally under their chins, but putting them in the tray return was the best.

MICHELLE TERRELL, b. 1969, archaeologist and historian

Sesame Street Wood Blocks
Playskool, Inc.
1975

Sesame Street Wood Blocks

One fact became increasingly clear as more and more families purchased televisions in the 1950s. For better or worse, kids were mesmerized by the glowing boxes. The cartoons, the live-action kids' shows, the westerns, the sitcoms, and yes, the commercials—all offered seemingly endless reasons for kids to remain glued to their spots in front of the tube.

As parents, educators, and other concerned adults fretted about the effect of television on children's minds, the idea of harnessing it as a means of educating children gained traction. Early shows, like *Mr. I. Magination* (1949–52), invited kids into a make-believe world where they learned about episodes in history. *Winky Dink and You* (1953–57) was an early attempt at interactive TV. Families purchased a "magic" screen of transparent plastic that affixed to their television screen. When prompted by Winky Dink's host, children entered into the show's action by drawing on their screens with special crayons. *Ding Dong School,* dubbed "the nursery school of the air," ran on NBC from 1952 to 1956 under the kindly tutelage of Miss Frances. And *Captain Kangaroo,* which aired for decades beginning in 1955, offered children tips on nutrition, reading, and more, interspersed with a steady stream of corny jokes and side-splitting sight gags, many involving the Captain's lovable sidekick, handyman Mr. Green Jeans.

There were also children's television shows on National Educational Television, a noncommercial public network established in 1954 and replaced in 1970 by Public Broadcasting Service (PBS). It was through this system of noncommercial TV that kids first encountered *Sesame Street,* the groundbreaking series that premiered on November 10, 1969. What made *Ses-*

Her friends knew her as Frances Rappaport Horwich, PhD. But to the children who tuned in to her popular *Ding Dong School* show every weekday on NBC, she was Miss Frances. Horwich was head of the department of education at what is now Roosevelt University in Chicago when her show debuted in 1952. Committed to engaging children at their level, Horwich began each program by looking directly into the camera and asking, "How are you this morning?" After pausing while her young viewers answered, she would respond with a warm affirmation. This simple yet groundbreaking approach has been applied by legions of children's television personalities, most notably Fred Rogers.

ame Street so special? According to Malcolm Gladwell, the show "was built around a single, breakthrough insight: that if you can hold the attention of children, you can educate them." *Sesame Street* incorporated an ambitious, measurable curriculum in a slick, attention-getting combination of puppets (Jim Henson's engaging Muppets), animation, live action, and topical humor. Kids were mesmerized, all right—not by a commercial for a glitzy toy, but by a cast of characters who spent their days rhapsodizing about numbers, letters, and desirable behavioral traits.

It should come as no surprise that this very successful series spawned very successful lines of toys. A succession of companies, including heavy hitters like Milton Bradley, Fisher-Price, and Playskool, licensed *Sesame Street* characters and created an endless stream of learning toys. Where *Sesame Street*'s production and ethos were cutting edge, though, the first toys associated with it were decidedly old school—hand puppets, plush animals, stacking toys, and building blocks. Playskool's alphabet blocks were made of wood, recalling the educational toys of earlier generations. "Can you tell me how to get to Sesame Street?" asked the show's theme song. In the 1970s, the route included a detour into some favorite toys of bygone generations.

Official Super Winky Dink Television Game Kit

Standard Toykraft Products, Inc.

1954

The original Winky Dink was a good seller for Standard Toykraft. But when the company tried to stage a comeback for its pixie-like character in 1969, the new version flopped, as parents heeded child-safety experts' warnings about radiation emitted by television screens.

Holly Hobbie
Knickerbocker Toy Company
1974

Holly Hobbie

When asked to name a memorable toy from the 1970s, many people pause, consider, then come up with something either electronic (think PONG, Atari, Electric Football) or futuristic (think *Star Wars*). But there were other hit toys as well, and one in particular was a conscious evocation of the past, in contrast to the flashing screens and space-age gadgetry of its contemporaries.

In 1966 Holly Ulinskas Hobbie, who had studied art education at Pratt Institute and painting at Boston University, submitted a portfolio of her work to American Greetings Corporation. Though the company didn't usually accept unsolicited art, they paired her paintings of a calico-clad girl with some homespun verses on a new line of greeting cards. Within a year Hobbie had a contract with American Greetings; by the 1970s her charming designs could be found on more than three hundred products, from wallpaper to dinnerware to nightgowns.

Enter Bob Childers, an American Greetings designer who believed that a doll was the next logical step for the Hobbie franchise. When his idea failed to get traction, he went home and stitched up a prototype. In 1974 Knickerbocker Toys licensed the Holly Hobbie character for a line of cloth dolls that evoked the wholesome charm of Raggedy Ann and other tried-and-true favorites. Soon Holly's entire family appeared in cloth form, from Baby Holly to Grandma Hobbie to friends Carrie, Heather, and Robby.

"While I have not deliberately tried to denote a specific time or person," Holly Ulinskas Hobbie once said, "my style and subjects bring back memories of a more tranquil and charming time period. For younger people, they seem to evoke 'the good old days' captured in books or on film . . . a time beyond memory." Whatever nostalgic yearnings were satisfied by Holly Hobbie were probably also met by NBC's *Little House on the Prairie*,

Holly's friend, Carrie

Lisa Meyers, right, and Amy Reinholdson

"

An excellent slice of history

I was given Holly Hobbie's friend Heather as a gift. She was among the three toys I chose to take with when we uprooted from Minnesota for a year and moved to Hawaii when I was eight years old. My friend's grandma also made the two of us matching prairie dresses and bonnets one Christmas. While pioneer popularity has waned, my daughters loved wearing the homemade dresses to the Laura Ingalls Wilder Pageant in Walnut Grove (Minnesota) two summers ago. It's an excellent slice of history that girls (young and old) help keep alive.

LISA MEYERS McCLINTICK, b. 1968, travel writer and photographer which ran for nine seasons beginning in 1974. Based on Laura Ingalls Wilder's books about her childhood, the series revolved around the adventures of a gingham-and-sunbonnet-clad heroine and her family. Every generation feels the push-pull of past and future, a longing for simpler times even as the promise of the new beckons. Holly, the Ingalls family, their neighbors, and even the sisters' nemesis, the conniving Nellie Oleson, drew children and adults into a hazy, pleasant past—as far, far away as a certain galaxy, and equally primed for some welcome escapism.

We made do with the knock-off Betsey Clark from Hallmark. Decoupaged the image from the store bags—free!

Pretty sure those pointy-headed Precious Moments babies are Betsey's direct descendants.

HEID E. ERDRICH, b. 1963, writer

Six Million Dollar Man

Kenner Products

1975–79

Six Million Dollar Man and Bionic Woman Action Figures

"We can rebuild him . . . we have the technology." So went the opening catchphrase of *The Six Million Dollar Man* television series, which told the story of Colonel Steve Austin, an astronaut who is "reassembled" with bionic body parts after a plane crash. Sporting a new left eye with zoom and infrared features, legs capable of running sixty miles per hour, and a right arm with the strength of a bulldozer, Austin is enlisted as a secret agent for the Office of Scientific Intelligence to battle evildoers around the globe. The TV series, starring Lee Majors in the leading role, was based on Martin Caidin's best-selling 1972 sci-fi novel *Cyborg;* it was a huge hit from 1974 to 1978 and spawned three made-for-television films and the spin-off series *The Bionic Woman,* which starred Lindsay Wagner as Austin's bionic gal pal Jaime Sommers.

The great success of both series was due in part to the inventive use of the robotic implants which made the characters "better . . . stronger . . . faster" and were demonstrated in slow motion with a synthesizer-esque sound effect that became a signature feature for the programs. Austin's and Sommers's arsenal of high-tech super-powered limbs and sensory organs (Sommers's bionic legs, right arm, and right ear were installed after a skydiving mishap) also made the heroes prime sources for a merchandising campaign that included everything from lunch boxes to bed sheets. Kenner marketed action figures for both characters, introducing Steve Austin to fans in 1975. Measuring thirteen inches high (over an inch taller than G.I. Joe), the jumpsuit-clad Austin sported his own accessories, including a telescopic eye with an eyepiece mounted in the back of his

Many an afternoon was spent running around the yard in slow motion, or rolling up the rubber "skin" of the Steve Austin action figure's arm to reveal the bionic implant underneath. (I once lost the implant and, distraught, wrote to Kenner Toys explaining my plight. Soon thereafter, an entire new bionic arm arrived in the mail. To date, this remains my best-ever experience with customer service.) I coveted the Oscar Goldman (Austin's boss) action figure, with his plaid jacket and briefcase full of very important papers.
SCOTT VON DOVIAK,
b. 1968, author

The exciting world of Jaime and Steve

Just like many longtime fans, I was a child of the '70s and was fortunate enough to be drawn into the exciting world of Jaime and Steve and the OSI. I always liked watching The Six Million Dollar Man, *but when I spotted a boy at school with the Steve Austin action figure and Back Pack Radio, it became my new favorite show (and I had to have one of those dolls). The debut of* The Bionic Woman *the following year was also a huge hit with me. Seeing the ads in the* TV Guide *would only build my excitement while waiting for Wednesday night. I saved the ad from the first* Bionic Woman *episode, and this became the start of my Bionic Woman collection.*

JAMES SHERRARD,
nonprofit coordinator

head, pliable skin on his right arm that could be peeled back to reveal mechanical parts, and "bionic strength" which, at the turn of the head and push of a button, allowed Steve to lift up to two pounds! Subsequent enhancements to the figure's mighty right arm included a "Bionic Grip" and a "Biosonic Arm" that could hack objects with brute force.

The success of the Austin action figure led to a plethora of accessories, play sets, and other figures, most notably the Bionic Woman doll, which debuted in 1976. Like her male counterpart, the Jaime Sommers figure had bionic components lurking beneath her "roll-back" rubber skin, and when she moved her head, Jaime's bionic ear would be activated with a series of clicks (reminiscent of the sound of Austin's right arm). Although the character of Jaime Sommers was fashioned as a nod to the 1970s empowered woman, the action figure embraced a more traditional gender role distinction, albeit with a "bionic" twist. Accessories included a "Mission Purse" stocked with wallet, money, ID, credit cards, makeup, and her mission assignment and Morse code decoder. Unlike miniature Steve, who got a lot of wear out of that red jumpsuit, little Jaime had a host of options from leisure suits to evening gowns thanks to the Bionic Woman Designer Collection. And while Steve recouped at his Bionic Transport and Repair Station, Jaime could freshen up at the Bionic Beauty Salon, complete with comb, brush, hair dryer, and bionics testing panel—what more could a super-powered woman need?

Speak & Spell
Texas Instruments
1976 and 1980

Little Professor and Speak & Spell

Educational toy. It's a term that intrigues adults and repels children. And yet, in the mid-1970s, Texas Instruments managed to introduce not one but two toys that proved attractive to both camps. How did this happen? It was all in the timing.

Ever since 1972, when Magnavox launched Odyssey, the first home video game system, electronic games were hot commodities. In 1976, Texas Instruments—best known for its grown-up calculators—introduced a hand-held game featuring a kindly professor. It was cute, it fit nicely in kids' hands, and it had a cutting-edge LED display. The fact that the display featured math problems was okay with kids and hugely appealing to adults. By riding the crest of the electronic toy wave, TI had found the sweet spot between fun and learning.

And that was just the beginning. Two years later, TI introduced Speak & Spell, which managed to cram a load of brandnew technology into an orange plastic shell small enough to fit in a kid's backpack. The Speak & Spell was fun because it actually talked to kids—and not in the way that Chatty Cathy and See 'n Say did, with a set of prerecorded phrases. Speak & Spell had an electronic voice that "spoke" words when prompted. The toy used a technology called digital signal processing, which converted the sound of the human voice into digital form. It marked the first time this technology—which TI had developed through its research into synthetic speech—had been used in a commercial product.

"The initial focus groups were interesting," recalled Richard Wiggins, a member of TI's development team. "It was never clear that they really understood how appealing a talking product would be to a small child." Sales took off, and soon the toy

> "One of my favorite toys from my childhood was Spell-It. I would spend hours picking out pictures or simple math problems on the board and then dialing the spelling of the words letter by letter, or doing the math problems. If I did it correctly, the right answer would show up in one of the four windows as if by magic. When I look back on it, this was sort of an early form of "computer." In the early days of no TV or very little TV, games like this were my indoor entertainment.
>
> CINDY CLARK, b. 1947, wife, mother, grandmother, and quilter

Decades before Texas Instruments entered the toy business, Cadaco-Ellis introduced an educational toy that used an ingenious system of rotating disks and magic windows to teach kids how to spell, add, subtract, and multiply.

was being exported to other countries, with the synthesized voice modified according to region. Alternate versions, such as Speak & Math and Speak & Read, were also introduced. But the real proof of TI's success arrived in 1982, when the adorable alien at the center of the blockbuster movie *E. T.* incorporated a 1978 version in his plan to phone home.

Spell-It
Cadaco-Ellis
1953

> *That was my favorite toy as a kid! Should have known that I would grow up to be a verbivore.*
>
> JESSICA ELLISON, b. 1979, history educator

Very early technology that obviously had its limitations

My brother and I would play with our Speak & Spell for as long as it took in one sitting for the internal "computer" to go all wacky on us and say funny things like "Spell xchdorngliesgphsf" (incomprehensible word in a funny scrambled computer voice) then we'd type in "xhsofhsecljfsidlbls" and it would say "That is incorrect" (or something like that) and we'd crack up and do it again, and again. Very early technology that obviously had its limitations.

SARAH JORDAN BEIMERS, b. 1966, historian

> *The Little Professor had a dull but loud mechanical voice, and I remember that it would flash three backwards "E's" if you did something wrong. The buttons were hard to press, too. But I remember great satisfaction when I got all ten questions right and the "10" would flash on the final screen. In the age before fancy computer games and apps, it seemed like a relatively exciting way to learn math skills compared to the rote memorization taking place in the classroom.*
>
> ALAYNA BOCKHEIM BLOOM, b. 1975, social studies teacher

Pet Rock

Rock Bottom Productions

1975

Pet Rock

Marketing is everything. Just ask Gary Dahl, inventor of the quintessential '70s fad, the Pet Rock. The idea came to the California advertising executive in 1975 while listening to a group of friends bemoan the rigors of pet ownership, like house training, walking, feeding, and grooming. Dahl joked about the ideal low-maintenance companion—a rock. Taking the joke seriously, he began crafting a business plan to sell the "pets" to consumers.

Dahl began by drafting a humorous owner's training manual, which contained instructions for teaching Pet Rock tricks like how to play dead and roll over, as well as how to potty train the rock. Owners were instructed to lay their Pet Rock "on some old newspapers. The rock will never know what the paper is for and will require no further instruction." Dahl sourced unadorned grey pebbles from a California construction supplier and packaged them in a cardboard box resembling an animal carrier, complete with ventilation holes and excelsior.

The Pet Rock debuted at the 1975 San Francisco gift show in August and then in New York, where the Neiman Marcus department store ordered five hundred. Dahl sent out his own press releases with amusing anecdotes like how the rocks were individually screened for obedience before being selected and packaged. The media had a field day with the story, and by Christmas nearly three-fourths of all the daily newspapers in America had published Pet Rock articles. Over five million rocks sold for $3.95 each within the first six months, making Gary Dahl a millionaire. The quick success of the Pet Rock spawned a host of copycat contenders, including a shrewdly marketed "Original Pet Rock"; and amenities like Pet Rock Obedience Lessons and Pet Rock Burial-at-Sea Services fueled the frenzy. Dahl worked hard to keep ahead of the competition by trying to sell his remaining Pet Rocks as Valentine's Day gifts for those

There are hundreds of breeds of rocks.

Of the hundreds of breeds of rocks known to man, only a few show the necessary aptitude required of a PET ROCK. The more important traits associated with genuine PET ROCKS are gentle disposition, eagerness to please, and a profound sense of responsibility.

Initial Training.

Nobody, but nobody likes a surly, misbehaving rock. Therefore, it is most important that you begin training immediately. Your PET ROCK should be made to know who is the boss, and that you will demand certain good manners and impeccable behavior if the two of you are to have a happy, well adjusted relationship.

A few of the more popular breeds.

Love me like a rock . . .

The thirty-page training manual accompanying the Pet Rock was the true genius behind Gary Dahl's concept. Dahl packed the handbook with jokes and puns that capitalized on the irony of having an inanimate object as a pet. Of course, owners were first instructed to name their rock, and then prepare comfortable quarters for the pet. The manual even suggested placing a ticking alarm clock next to the rock to soothe its nerves upon arrival in its new surroundings. To entertain their new pet, owners could include the rock in activities like watching television, playing video games, or going on walks. The manual also included commands that could be taught to the new pet. While "sit" and "stay" were relatively simple to learn, "roll over" usually required additional input from the owner. "Come" was discovered to be virtually impossible for the rock to master.

Greta Bahnemann in red shirt

in need of a stress-free companion, but by early 1976 the fad had fizzled.

Although the Pet Rock, like most fads, was short lived, it cemented Gary Dahl's reputation as one of the great creative geniuses of the baby boom era. But what was the attraction? Was it more than just an amusing gag gift? Inventor Ken Hakuta claims that crazes like the Pet Rock are a therapeutic diversion from the stresses of daily life. "If there were more fads," Hakuta observed, "there would probably be a lot fewer psychiatrists . . . Instead of paying $100-an-hour therapy sessions, you could just get yourself a couple of Wacky Wallwalkers and a Slinky and lock yourself up in a room for a couple of hours. When you came out, you'd be fine."

What higher praise could there be for a Pet Rock?

I really wanted one of these (hey, I was seven), but my parents refused to buy me one . . . something about being a matter of principle ("Rocks are free!"). So I caught a "wild rock" on the North Shore of Lake Superior and brought it home. I made a home for my wild rock in a shoe box (complete with shredded newspaper). But eventually, I realized you just can't tame a wild thing . . . and I set it free.
GRETA BAHNEMANN, b. 1969, academic librarian

***Star Wars* Action Figures**
Kenner Products
1978

Star Wars Action Figures

When George Lucas's sci-fi epic *Star Wars* hit theaters in May of 1977, America was in the throes of a downward spiral of disappointment and disillusion. The carnage of the Vietnam War, which ended in 1975, was still raw, as was the Watergate scandal, which prompted the resignation of President Richard Nixon in 1974 and raised the public's distrust of government to new heights. The U.S. economy was also suffering from a mid-decade recession, yearly inflation, escalating unemployment, and rising energy prices. Americans were grasping for hope, a renewed confidence in our leaders, and a universal sense of pride in being Americans.

With its archetypical characters, classic struggle of good versus evil, and astonishing special effects, *Star Wars* was just the tonic required to unify a crestfallen nation and raise its collective spirits. The film had an expressly powerful impact on Lucas's target audience—America's youth. "There's a whole generation growing up without any kind of fairy tales," said Lucas. "And kids need fairy tales. It's an important thing for society to have for kids." Lucas understood the significance of creating compelling characters to embody those tales, from the Jedi war hero Luke Skywalker to the malevolent Darth Vader to the plucky droid R2-D2. The young director also recognized the market potential of these characters and wisely acquired the merchandising rights to the film from Twentieth Century Fox, a decision the studio would sorely regret.

When *Star Wars* became an instant smash hit, grossing over $220 million during its initial theatrical run, the executives at Twentieth Century Fox were not the only ones kicking themselves. Mego Corporation, the leading maker of action figures

> *I was nineteen when the first* Star Wars *movie came out in '77. During this period of time, superheroes had became more popular, more generic, and less interesting to me. I shifted my attention to the fantasy genre. I was trying to find my way as a young adult in a post-Watergate world of urban decay, high unemployment, and high interest rates. The future looked bleak.*
>
> *The release of* Star Wars *was an exciting contrast to the times and filled my need for an archetypal story of the "hero's journey," Oedipal conflicts, and mythical figures on epic quests.* Star Wars *provided me with the comfort of the familiar and the freshness of science fiction fantasy—and had ground-breaking special effects! The* Star Wars *mantra "May the Force be with you" was powerful for me during these difficult times.*

STEPHEN YOGI RUEFF, b. 1958, business consultant to cultural nonprofits

in the 1970s, had passed on the license for *Star Wars* figures, a golden opportunity which was picked up by Kenner Products. But the Cincinnati-based toy maker was unprepared for the film's galactic success and failed to produce sufficient inventory for the holiday season. Instead, an "Early Bird Certificate Package" was sold containing a voucher that could be redeemed for four *Star Wars* action figures. When the first four figures—Luke Skywalker, Princess Leia Organa, R2-D2, and Chewbacca—debuted, they were less than four inches tall, the result of a cost-saving measure imposed on plastic manufacturers by the 1970s oil crisis. Yet despite their diminutive stature (which became the new standard for action figures) and limited articulation (they only moved at the hips, shoulders, and neck), the demand for the figures was astounding, and eight additional characters were promptly introduced: Darth Vader, Han Solo, Ben (Obi-Wan) Kenobi, C-3PO, Stormtrooper, Jawa, Sand People, and Death Squad Commander. Kenner continued to expand the *Star Wars* line with additional figures, vehicles, and play set accessories, and by 1978 over 40 million units had been gobbled up by eager fans. With the release of each film sequel, the *Star Wars* inventory grew, and by 1984 Kenner had designed seventy-nine unique characters for the market. Although Kenner discontinued the production of *Star Wars* figures in 1985, the captivating spell of "the Force"—and these figures—continues to be with fans young and old alike.

| JAWA | STORMTROOPER | DEATH SQUAD COMMANDER | SEE THREEPIO | DARTH VADER | BEN KENOBI | SAND PEOPLE | LUKE SKYWALKER | CHEWBACCA | HAN SOLO | PRINCESS LEIA | ARTOO DETOO |

"The Twelve"

I'll never forget finally finding a Sand Person figure while on vacation in Oklahoma. There was ONE left and a younger boy was holding it and pleading with his mom to buy it for him. Luckily for me, his mom said no and the prized figure was placed back on the shelf. I held on to that figure so tightly all the way to the cash register that, if I remember correctly through the haze of nostalgia, it had to be surgically removed from my hands before I could open him and add him to my growing Star Wars figure ranks. That was a good day. When the Jawa finally appeared in stores, most of us were very surprised to see that he no longer sported the vinyl cape that we had seen in so many promotional photos on the back of packages and in pack-in booklets. He was wearing a soft cloth hooded robe which seemed very odd at the time, given the nature of the previous eleven figures' vinyl capes and robes. Plus, it hid the Jawa's trademark bandoliers that were part of the base figure's sculpt. Ah, but it was good to finally complete "The Twelve."

BRIAN ASHMORE, illustrator

I turned ten the summer that Star Wars came out. My younger brother, Matt, and I must have seen the movie more than a half dozen times that year and probably drove our parents crazy with our love of everything Star Wars. For Christmas the toys to get that year were Star Wars action figures. Unfortunately, the demand was so great that the manufacturer couldn't get the toys on the shelves by Christmas. What was offered instead was a special "Early Bird" holiday package that included a cardboard display for the action figures, with a couple of trading cards and a Star Wars Space Club membership card attached, and a coupon for four action figures: Luke, Princess Leia, Chewbacca, and Artoo Detoo. I don't remember now if I was disappointed at not receiving actual toys, but I do remember spending hours staring at the drawings of the action figures on the background of the cardboard display and dreaming about what it would be like to have all of the figures.

WILLIAM BECKER, b. 1967,

U.S. Navy scientist

William Becker, standing, with brother Matt

Simon
Milton Bradley Company
1978

Simon

It seems so simple. The flying saucer–shaped toy plays a musical sequence that you repeat by pressing colored buttons. Success leads to longer sequences. Go with the flow, and you're fine. But if you think too hard, you'll lose focus and hear the electronic RAZZ signaling "game over."

On May 15, 1978, Milton Bradley introduced Simon at a glitzy party at New York City's Studio 54 nightclub. It was an instant hit, ushering in a brave new world of handheld electronic games. There had been a few earlier successes—Mattel Auto Race, anyone?—but nothing had the appeal or the staying power of Simon. By the end of 1982, after just four years on the market, more than ten million copies had been sold.

The game that requires more intuition than thought was the result of some serious thinking on the part of inventors Ralph Baer and Howard Morrison. Baer's day job was chief engineer at a military electronics development company. In his spare time, though, he was fascinated by electronic game design. He created Magnavox's Odyssey, the first home video game system, which was introduced in 1972. Morrison was a toy designer who worked for Marvin Glass and Associates, an industry giant responsible for dozens of hits, from Mouse Trap to Lite Brite.

Fast-forward to 1976, when Baer visited a trade show where he played an Atari arcade game that required him to repeat a sequence of tones. "Nice gameplay. Terrible execution," Baer recalled. "Visually boring. Miserable, rasping sounds." Baer and Morrison took the essence of the arcade game and turned it into a handheld game they first called Follow Me.

Baer knew that if players were going to stick with his game, he'd need to improve on the "rasping sounds" of its Atari precursor. Baer thumbed through a children's musical dictionary and found the bugle, which plays only four harmonious tones.

> **I still have mine and it works—
> and I still can't beat it at Level 4!**
>
> *As I recall, I saved up my money until I could afford to buy it for around
> $25, which was a lot at that time. It was addictive; once you got going
> and were up to repeating the sequences for long stretches of time, you'd
> be so focused the house could have burnt down around you. My best
> successes came when I played it like a musical instrument, recalling
> the tones instead of the color/light patterns.*
>
> DIANE MADIR, b. 1966, technician

Baer and Morrison took their melodious model to Milton Bradley. The company loved the concept, but the name needed work. They tried several, including Tap Me and Feedback, before they named their futuristic game after an enduring classic, the children's game Simon Says.

"It's the things we play with and the people who help us play that make a great difference in our lives."
— Mr. Rogers

Image and Source Credits

Unless otherwise noted, all objects in Minnesota Historical Society collections. Photography by Jason Onerheim.

Unless otherwise noted, all reminiscences and childhood photographs supplied by contributors and used with permission.

All trademarks are the property of their respective owners. See page 210 for details.

page 17	Fran Schaper quoted in Minneapolis *Star Tribune*, November 28, 1998
page 18	Minnesota Historical Society collections, ID GV8.8 p4
page 26	Dr. Stephen Chu biography at NobelPrize.org
pages 28–29	View-Master loaned by Kate Roberts
pages 32–33	Betsy McCall Paper Dolls loaned by Mary Pat Roberts
page 36	Sweet Sue loaned by Janet Peterson Lee
pages 40, 42	Raggedy Ann, Raggedy Andy, and book loaned by Karen Annexstad Humphrey
pages 48, 50–51	All Hot Wheels items loaned by David Barnhill
pages 48, 49	All Matchbox cars loaned by Jane Leonard
pages 56, 59	Sikorsky Helicopter loaned by Gary Hofmeister
page 66	photo courtesy of *The Unforgettable Buzz*
page 71	Mike Smith quote from Mike Smith Enterprises Blog, January 29, 2011
pages 90, 92, 93	Barbie, Ken, and car loaned by Lory Sutton
pages 91, 92	Connie Quinn and Janice Fisher quotes from "Readers Share More Barbie Memories," Richmond, Virginia, *Times-Dispatch*, March 8, 2009
page 92	Kathy Bunkley quote from "Still Fabulous at 50: Readers Share Personal Barbie Stories," Abilene, Texas, *Reporter News*, March 8, 2009

page 93	Barbie Teen-age Fashion Model courtesy of the Strong™, Rochester, New York, February 19, 2014
page 96	Artwork Copyright © and ™ Rube Goldberg Inc. All Rights Reserved. RUBE GOLDBERG ® is a registered trademark of Rube Goldberg Inc. All materials used with permission. rubegoldberg.com.
pages 98, 99, 101	Thingmaker loaned by David Barnhill
pages 112–13	Edward Green quote from "History of Tonka Trucks," *Truckers Report,* available: thetruckersreport.com
page 116	Frisbie pie tin courtesy of the Strong™, Rochester, New York, February 19, 2014
page 117	Frisbee photo courtesy of the Strong™, Rochester, New York, March 14, 2014
page 124	photo courtesy St. Paul Pioneer Press/Buzz Magnuson
page 136	Big Wheel photo courtesy of the Strong™, Rochester, New York, March 14, 2014
page 149	Taige Crenshaw quote from taigecrenshaw.com, July 26, 2010
pages 154, 157	Play Family Castle loaned by Peg Olson
page 160	Sherri Gardner Howell quote from "Bicycles Help Spin Nostalgic Memories," *Knoxville (Tennessee) News Sentinel,* August 10, 2012
page 173	Jeff Hage quote used with permission from the *Fergus Falls (Minnesota) Daily Journal*
	Scott DeSmit quote from "A Baby Boomer's Take on Classic Toys," *The Daily News* (Genesee, Wyoming, and Orleans counties, New York), October 12, 2013
page 180	Frances Horwich photo courtesy Wikimedia Commons

Toy Trademarks

COOTIE, MOUSE TRAP, EASY-BAKE OVEN, TONKA, G.I. JOE, TWISTER, SPIROGRAPH, NERF, and SIMON are all registered trademarks of Hasbro, Inc.

AMERICAN FLYER is a registered trademark of Lionel, LLC.

ERECTOR is a registered trademark of Meccano S.N.

VIEW-MASTER, MATCHBOX, BARBIE and KEN, UNO, and LITTLE PEOPLE are all registered trademarks of Mattel, Inc.

RAGGEDY ANN and ANDY and associated characters are trademarks of Simon & Schuster, Inc. RAGGEDY ANN is a trademark of Hasbro, Inc.

REVELL is a registered trademark of Revell, Inc.

PLAYSKOOL is a registered trademark of Playskool, Inc.

CREEPY CRAWLERS is a registered trademark of JAKKS Pacific, Inc.

RAT FINK and associated characters are trademarks of the Estate of Edward Roth, Inc.

FRISBEE is a registered trademark of WHAM-O, Inc.

BIG WHEEL is a registered trademark of Alpha International, Inc.

GREEN MACHINE is a registered trademark of Huffy Corporation.

JARTS is a registered trademark of Poof-Slinky Fundex, LLC.

SESAME STREET, its logo, and associated characters are trademarks of Sesame Workshop.

HOLLY HOBBIE is a registered trademark of Those Characters From Cleveland, Inc.

BIONIC WOMAN is a registered trademark of Universal City Studios, LLLP.

SPEAK & SPELL and LITTLE PROFESSOR are registered trademarks of Texas Instruments, Inc.

STAR WARS and associated characters are registered trademarks of Lucasfilm Entertainment Company LTD.

All other trademarks are the property of their respective owners.

Acknowledgments

Thanks to our colleagues for the help in creating this book—

Tom Braun
Nicole Delfino Jansen
Earl Gutnik
Ian Lilligren
Jason Onerheim
Jack Rumpel
Tom Warn

Mali Collins
Robert J. Smith III

Dan Leary
Pam McClanahan
Shannon Pennefeather

Index

A

Abakanowicz, Bruno, 127
A. C. Gilbert Company, 20–27
action figures, 118–21, 186–89, 198–201
Aiyawar, Ann-Marie, 160
Akeman, Ed, 149
All in the Family, 145
All-Star Electric Football Game, 64–67
Alpha-1 Ballistic Missile, 68–71
American Bandstand, 14–15, 107
American Character Doll Company, 36–39
American Flyer Trains, 20–23
American Greetings Corporation, 183
American Plastic (Meikle), 45–46
AMSCO Industries, Inc., 68–71
Anderson, Lisa Crawford, 165
Annexstad, Eleanor Schwartau, 40, 43
Apple Computer Company, 146
Archie Bunker, 145–46
Ashmore, Brian, 201
Asimov, Isaac, 87–88
Atari, 203

Baby (Brother) Tender Love, 150–53
Baby and Child Care (Spock), 63
Baer, Ralph, 203, 205

Bahnemann, Greta, 197
Baker, Lynn, 111
Barbie, 90–93
Beatles, 80
Becker, William, 201
Beimers, Sarah Jordan, 193
Bethune, Mary McLeod, 141
Betsy McCall Paper Dolls, 32–35
Betty Crocker, 105
Beulah, 139
bicycles, 158–61
Big Wheel, 134–37
Bild Lilli doll, 91
Bionic Woman action figure, 186–89
blocks, Sesame Street wood, 178–80
Bloom, Alayna Bockheim, 193
Boone, Daniel, 54
Branwyn, Gareth, 168
Britt, Debra, 140
Brookglad Corporation, 72–75
Brown, Helen Gurley, 79
Brown v. Board of Education, 13
Bunche, Ralph, 141
Bunkley, Kathy, 92
Burke, Jerry, 69
Burlingame, Sheila, 141
Burns, Edgar, 99

Cadaco-Ellis, 192
Caidin, Martin, 187

Cape Canaveral Erector Set, 24
Captain Kangaroo, 18, 179
Car Craft magazine, 107
Carlin, George, 146
Carroll, Diahann, 139–40
cars, 48–51
Carson, Johnny, 123
Carson, Rachel, 80
"Century of Toys" list, 18
Chatty Cathy, 151
Childers, Bob, 183
Child Protection and Toy Safety Act, 163, 172
Children at Play (Chudacoff), 6
Chudacoff, Howard, 6
Clark, Cindy, 191
Clark, Dick, 14, 107
Cold War, 12–13
Consumer Product Safety Commission, 137, 163–64
Coonskin Cap, Davy Crockett, 52–55
Cootie, Game of, 16–19
Cox, Fred, 171
Creasey, Karen, 104
Creech, Sara Lee, 141
Creepy Crawlers, 99
Crenshaw, Taige, 149
Crockett, Davy, 52–53
Cross, Gary, 175
Crounse, Avery, 111
Cyborg (Caidin), 187

Dahl, Gary, 195–97
Dam, Thomas, 83
Dam Things Entertainment, 83–85
Davy Crockett Coonskin Cap,
    52–55
Dayton's, 17
Design-O-Marx, 129
Desmit, Scott, 173
Ding Dong School, 179–80
Disney, Walt, 80
Disneyland, 14
dolls, 32–35, 40–43, 72–75, 90–93,
    138–41, 150–53, 182–85
Dr. Doolittle See 'n Say, 130

Eames, Charles, 15
Earth Day, 144, 169
Easy-Bake Oven, 102–5
Easy Rider, 135, 137
Ebony, 139–40
Eckberg, Jim, 89
Edison, Thomas, 131
Edmonds-Metzel Manufacturing
    Company, 21
Eisenhower, Dwight, 14, 78
Ellison, Jessica, 193
Erdrich, Heid E., 185
Erector Set, 21, 24–27

Fair Lady bicycle, 160–61
FAUNI-trolls, 83
The Feminine Mystique (Friedan),
    13
Fisher, Denys, 127

Fisher, Herman, 155
Fisher, Janice, 92
Fisher-Price Toys, 154–57
Foley, Charles F., 123, 124, 125
Football Game, All-Star Electric,
    64–67
Ford, Gerald, 145, 167
Frank, Gill, 145
Franscioni, Warren, 115
Fraser, Antonia, 3
Free to Be You and Me, 176
Friedan, Betty, 13
Frisbee, 114–17
Frisbie Baking Company, 115, 116

Gabor, Eva, 123
Game of Cootie, 16–19
Garcia, Roddy, 66
Gebert Fuller, Sherri, 101
General Mills, 105
George Jefferson, 145–46
George S. Bailey Hat Company,
    52–55
G. I. Joe, 118–21
Gilbert, Alfred Carlton, 21–27
Gilbert, Alfred Jr., 22, 27
Gladwell, Malcolm, 180
Glaser, Lewis, 57
Glass, Marvin, 95
Godey's Lady's Book, 33
Goldberg, Rube, 95–96
Gotham Pressed Steel Corpora-
    tion, 64
Grabitske, David M., 136
Graham, Anne, 164
Graves, Harold, 29
Green, Carissa, 19
Green, Edward, 112–13
The Green Machine, 137

Growing Up Skipper, 153
Gruber, William, 29
Gruelle, Johnny, 41–42
Gruelle, Marcella Delight, 41
Guyer, Reyn, 123–25, 171

Hage, Jeff, 173
Hakuta, Ken, 197
Halsom Products, 61
Handler, Elliot, 50
Handler, Ruth, 91–93
Happy Meal, 147
Hasbro, Inc., 18, 42, 118–21
Headrick, Eddie, 115
Heiber, Bob, 17
Henson, Jim, 180
Hier, Daryle W., 66
A History of Toys (Fraser), 3
Hobbie, Holly Ulinskas, 183
Hofmeister, Gary, 58
Holgate Brothers, 61
Holly Hobbie, 182–85
Hoon, Dianne Becker, 35
Horsman Dolls, 75
Horwich, Frances Rappaport, 180
Hot Stuff, 144
Hot Wheels cars, 50–51
Howard, Kenny "Von Dutch," 159
Howell, Sherri Gardner, 160
Hula-Hoop, 117, 123
Humphrey, Karen Annexstad, 43
Hurston, Zora Neale, 141

Ideal Toy Corporation, 86–89,
    94–97, 141
Ike-A-Doo Krazy Ikes Game, 44–47

International Games, Inc., 148–49
Ives, Burl, 167

Jaime Sommers, 187–88
Jarts, 162–65
Jarts Company, 162
The Jeffersons, 145–46
The Jetsons, 78–79
J. L. Wright Company, 61
Jobs, Steve, 146
Johnny Horizon Environmental Test Kit, 166–69
John Schroeder Lumber Company, 61
Johnson, Lyndon B., 79
Johnson, Patrice M., 152
Johnson, Yvonne (Dugas), 37
Julia, 139
Julia doll, 138–41

Kendall, Karen Vaughan, 31
Ken doll, 90–93, 120
Kenner Products, 102–5, 126–29, 186–89, 198–201
Khrushchev, Nikita, 12
Kid's Stuff (Cross), 175
Kleppe, Thomas, 169
Klick, Richard, 22, 31
Knapp Electric Company, 45
Knerr, Richard, 115
Knickerbocker Toy Company, 42, 182–85
Krazy Ikes, 44–47
Kroc, Ray, 14
Krushchev, Nikita, 12, 15
Kubrick, Stanley, 80

Kustom Kulture, 159
Kuuskoski, Helena and Martti, 83

Ladies' Home Journal, 33–34
Lavaque, Jackie, 127
Learn How Dagwood Splits the Atom! (Musial), 163
Lee, Janet Peterson, 39
Leonard, Jane, 51
Lesney Products, 48, 49
Levine, Don, 119
Lil' Chik Bicycle, 158–61
Lilli doll, 91
Lionel, 21–22
Lipp, Kelly, 157
Little House on the Prairie, 183–85
"Little People," 155–56
Little Professor, 190–93
Locke, John, 3
Lohr, Ray, 135
Louis Marx & Company, 134–37
Lucas, George, 199

Madir, Diane, 204
Marx, Louis, 129
Matchbox cars, 48–51
Mattel, Inc., 48, 50, 90–93, 98–101, 130–33, 138–41, 150–53
Mattox, John, 171
McBurrows, Annuel, 140
McCall's, 33–35
McCarthy, Joseph, 12
McClintick, Lisa Meyers, 184
McDonald's, 14, 147
McDonald's Familiar Places play set, 174–77
Meikle, Jeffrey, 45–46

Melin, Arthur "Spud," 115
Meyers, Lisa, 184
Mickey Mouse, 107
Mighty Tonka Crane and Clam, 110–11
Milk, Harvey, 147
Miller, Gary Frank, 120
Milliorn, Mark, 117
Milton Bradley Company, 122–25, 202–5
Mintz, Steven, 8
Miss America beauty pageant, 81
Monroe, Marilyn, 13
Montessori, Maria, 8
Morrison, Howard, 203, 205
Morrison, Walter "Fred," 115
Mouse Trap, 94–97
Mr. I. Magination, 179
Muppets, 180
Mysto, 25

National Aeronautics and Space Administration (NASA), 15
National Football League (NFL), 67
NERF ball, 170–73
Nixon, Richard, 12–13, 15, 145, 163, 199

Ockuly, Jim, 67, 164
Odell, Jack, 49
Odyssey, 191, 203
Official Super Winky Dink Television Game Kit, 179, 181
Olson, Elizabeth, 140
Olson, Peg Walter, 157

Paper Dolls, Betsy McCall, 32–35
Parker, Fess, 53–54
Parker Brothers, 166–73
patents, 17, 41, 115, 125
Payne, Lee, 65, 67
Peanuts comic strip, 167
Pet Rock, 194–97
Piaget, Jean, 8
Play Family Castle, 154–57
Playskool, 42, 60–61, 174–80
Pluto Platter, 115
Poor, Pitiful Pearl, 72–75
Precision Specialties, 57
Price, Irving, 155

Queasy Bake Cookerator, 105
Quinn, Connie, 91

Rabens, Neil, 123, 124, 125
Ragan, Mac, 51
Raggedy Ann and Andy, 40–43
Raggedy Ann Stories (Gruelle), 41–43
Rasmussen, Boyd, 167
Rat Fink, 59, 106–9
Register, Cheri, 47
Reinholdson, Amy, 184
Revell Company, 56–59, 106–9
Rich, Mark, 2, 8
Robbins, Merle, 149
Robot Commando, 86–89
Rock Bottom Productions, 194–97
Roe v. Wade, 145
Rogers, Fred, 180, 206
Roosevelt, Eleanor, 141

Rotate-O-Matic Super Astronaut, 88
Roth, Ed "Big Daddy," 59, 107–9, 159
Rousseau, Jean-Jacques, 5
Roysdon, Keith, 101
Rube Goldberg, 95–96
Rueff, Stephen Yogi, 109, 200
"Runaround" (Asimov), 88

Sara Lee doll, 141
Sas, Norman, 65
Saturday Night Live, 146
Saturday Review, 139
Sawyer's, Inc., 28–31
Schaper, Fran, 17
Schaper, William Herbert, 17–18
Scheller, Terry, 97
Schwinn Bicycle Company, 158–61
Scott-Heron, Gil, 81
Sears Wish Book, 2
See 'n Say, 130–33
Sesame Street, 176, 179–80
Sesame Street wood blocks, 178–80
Sex and the Single Girl (Brown), 79
Shayon, Robert Lewis, 139
Sherman, Rose, 7
Sherrard, James, 188
Shores, Earl, 66
Shrek! (Steig), 73
Sikorsky H-19 Rescue Helicopter, 56–59
Silent Spring (Carson), 80
Simon, 202–5
Six Million Dollar Man action figure, 186–89
Skaneateles Train and Track Set, 60–63
Smith, Leslie and Rodney, 49

Smith, Mike, 71
Speak & Spell, 190–93
Spell-It, 191–92
Spielberg, Steven, 55
Spirograph, 126–29
Spock, Benjamin, 63
Sputnik, 71, 87
Squirtles, 100
Standard Toykraft Products, Inc., 181
Stanfield-Hagert, Annie, 75
Star Wars action figures, 198–201
Steig, William, 73
Steve Austin, 187–88
Stewart, Martie Goltz, 85
Sting-Ray bicycle, 159–61
The Story of G. I. Joe, 119
Super Bowl, 81
Sutton-Smith, Brian, 61
Sweet Sue, 36–39
Sylvester and the Magic Pebble (Steig), 73

Terrell, Eva, 104
Terrell, Michelle, 177
Tesch, Alvin, 111
Texaco Experiment, Inc., 69
Texas Instruments, 190–93
Tezak, Robert, 149
Thingmaker, 98–101
Tonight Show, 123
Tonka Trucks, 110–13
Toy Industry Association, 18
Toy Manufacturers Association, 163
Toy Safety Committee, 163
Toys and Culture (Sutton-Smith), 61
trains, 20–23, 60–63

Trolls, 82–85
Tru-Vue, 29
Tudor Metal Products, 65–67
Twister, 122–25

Ultimate Frisbee, 115–16
Uneeda Doll Company, 85
The Unforgettable Buzz (Shores, Garcia), 66
Uno, 148–49
U.S. Consumer Product Safety Commission, 137, 163–64

View-Master, 28–31
Von Doviak, Scott, 187

Walt Disney Studios, 29–30
Warman's 101 Greatest Baby Boomer Toys (Rich), 2
Waters, Ethel, 139
Weathermac Corporation, 52–55
Wham-O, 114–17
Whitman Publishing Company, 44–47
W. H. Schaper Manufacturing Company, Inc., 16–19
Wiggins, Richard, 191

Wilson, Sloan, 71
Winky Dink and You, 179
Winky Dink Television Game Kit, Official Super, 179, 181
Women's Army Corps, 147
Woolworth's, 78
World War I, 17
World War II, 6, 12, 26–27, 29, 45, 57, 119
Wozniak, Steve, 146
Wright, Mark, 121
Wright, Ralph, 189

Young, Sheila, 33

Toys of the '50s, '60s and '70s was designed by Mind*Spark Creative.

Layout and typesetting by Judy Gilats in St. Paul, Minnesota.

The book was printed at Friesens Corporation in Altona, Manitoba, Canada.